QUARTERNARY ESSAYS

QUATERNARY ESSAYS

*applying Shakespeare's nature-based
Sonnet philosophy to life and art*

ROGER PETERS

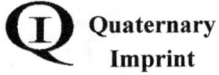
Quaternary
Imprint

Quaternary Essays
*applying Shakespeare's nature-based
Sonnet philosophy to life and art*

is a companion volume to *William Shakespeare's Sonnet Philosophy*
Volumes 1, 2, 3 and 4 published as a set in 2005 (republished 2019).
Shakespeare's Global Philosophy 2017
Shakespeare & Mature Love 2017
Shakespeare's Philosophy Illustrated 2018
All published by Quaternary Imprint

Copyright © 2020 Roger Peters
All rights reserved.

This book may not be reproduced, in whole or in part, including illustrations, stored in a retrieval system, or transmitted in any form or by any means without the prior permission in writing of Quaternary Imprint or as expressly permitted by law, or under terms agreed by the appropriate reprographic rights organizations. The book must not be circulated in any other binding or cover.

ISBN 978-0-473-55446-0 (pbk)
ISBN 978-0-473-55447-7 (hbk)

Page setup by Maree Horner

Quaternary Imprint
Published for the Quaternary Institute
www.quaternaryinstitute.com

Maree

Other titles by Roger Peters

William Shakespeare's Sonnet Philosophy
(Four volume, slipcase set - 2005)

Volume 1
How Shakespeare structures
his nature-based philosophy into the *Sonnets*
before he publishes them in 1609
(*Volume 1,* second edition - 2019)

Volume 2
A line by line analysis
of the 154 individual sonnets using
the *Sonnet* philosophy
as the basis for their meaning
(*Volume 2,* second edition - 2018)

Volume 3
An analysis of individual plays and poems
to show that the *Sonnet* philosophy
is the basis for their meaning
(*Volume 3,* second edition - 2020)

Volume 4
How the works of
Wittgenstein, Duchamp, and Mallarmé
led to an appreciation
of Shakespeare's philosophy
(*Volume 4,* second edition - 2019)

Shakespeare's Global Philosophy (2017)
exploring Shakespeare's nature-based
philosophy in the sonnets, plays and Globe

Shakespeare & Mature Love (2017)
how to get from nature to love in Shakespeare

Shakespeare's Philosophy Illustrated (2018)
Quaternary teaching aids

QUATERNARY IMPRINT
Published for the Quaternary Institute

CONTENTS

Preface

Introduction i

How to Use the Nature template 1

    Preamble – Shakespeare's nature-based philosophy   3

    1. Philosophy versus Psychology   10

    2. Nature versus God   15

    3. Sexual versus Erotic   19

    4. Technocratic mind-sets   23

    5. Christ the Carpenter   28

    6. Non-linear and Linear   32

    7. Fact versus Fiction   37

    8. Sex versus Gender   41

    9. Reverse Psychology   46

    10. Conclusion   60

From Male to Female: where the default lies 63

Shakespeare and Democracy 73

From Tertiary to Quaternary 91

    The Creative University   93

    Criteria for Quaternary   113

    Quaternary Pedagogy   125

    Upgrading from Tertiary to Quaternary   133

Preface

Quaternary Essays celebrates, in part, the founding of the Quaternary Institute twenty years ago in 2000 at the turn of the Millennium. The Quaternary Institute website *www.quaternaryinstutute.com* was established at the same time and Quaternary Imprint followed soon after with the publication in 2005 of the four-volume 1760-page slip-case set *William Shakespeare's Sonnet Philosophy*.

For the first time in 400 years an appreciation of Shakespeare's consistent and comprehensivenature-based philosophy published by him in the 1609 *Sonnets* as the basis for the thirty-six plays in the 1623 *Folio* and his four longer poems is now available for a post-Tertiary audience. After all, Tertiary has failed completely over those 400 years to come anywhere near understanding Shakespeare's natural philosophy.

Following twenty-five years from the late 1960s of studying proto-Quaternary thinkers, scientists and artists, in 1995 at a reading of the whole set of 154 sonnets it was apparent they contained a breathtakingly significant breakthrough past the diversionary apologetics that constitutes current Tertiary pedagogy and research. Now, in 2020, the investigative phase of the Quaternary pedagogical and publishing enterprise is nearing completion.

A summary Volume *Shakespeare's Global Philosophy* was published in 2017, an essay on *Shakespeare & Mature Love* in 2018, and a pictorial Volume *Shakespeare's Philosophy Illustrated* in 2019. Now with the completion in May this year of an 800,000-word commentary around a facsimile of the 1623 *Folio* and this Volume brings together essays written at various times over the preceding ten years.

In preparation for publication is a Volume titled *ACQUITTAS or The Assize Court for the Quaternary Investigation of Tertiary Travesties Against Shakespeare*, examining the literary crimes perpetrated on the works of Shakespeare over the last 400 years.

Introduction

Preamble

William Shakespeare (1564-1616) wrote thirty-six plays, which his colleagues Heminge and Condell publish in the 1623 *Folio*, he oversees the publication of the 154 sonnets in 1609 as *Shake-speares Sonnets* and publishes four longer poems in 1593, 1594, 1601 and 1609. In the process, he creates hundreds of characters in a complexity of situations and life experiences in the plays and poems and a group of generic characters in the sonnets that still resonate with the modern mind.

Shakespeare's ability to write dramas and verse both relevant to his own day and still very pertinent in ours is a consequence of the consistent and comprehensive nature-based philosophy that informs all his works and which he presents deliberately in the logically structured set of 154 sonnets.

These essays – and the others essays published in the four-volume set *William Shakespeare's Sonnet Philosophy* (2005 & republished 2019) – consider a variety of issues examined and made palpable by the application of Shakespeare's unprecedented articulation of the birthright philosophy of humankind in the 1609 *Sonnets*.

Deriving the Nature template from the 1609 Sonnets

While the derivation of Shakespeare's consistent and comprehensive nature-based philosophy from the 1609 Sonnets is explained and detailed at length in Volumes 1 and 2 of *William Shakespeare's Sonnet Philosophy* and in the first Part of *Shakespeare's Global Philosophy* (2017), for the purposes of these essays a brief account seems appropriate.

Because the *Sonnet* philosophy is the only interpretative tool required to appreciate all Shakespeare's works and their implications for every aspect of human thought and expression, the sound isomorphic structuring of the nature/female/male and the body/mind relationship throughout the sonnet set is worth revisiting.

The logical arrangement of the 154 sonnets is readily apparent in the biological/logical structuring of the whole set and its dedicated sequences and groups. The 154 sonnets represent nature with 28 sonnets representing the Mistress or female and 126 sonnets representing the Master Mistress or male with the consequent groups representing increase or procreation and beauty and truth or sensations and language. The *Nature template – Sonnets* below shows the natural relationships in diagrammatic form.

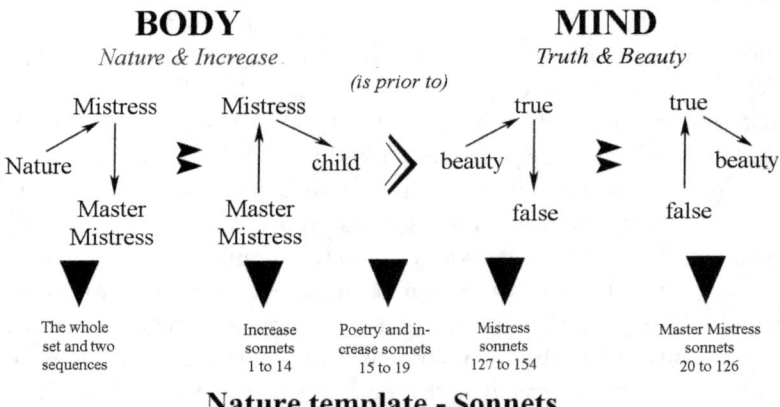

Nature template - Sonnets

The *Nature template* can also be presented using generic words to represent each of Shakespeare's more evocative *Sonnet* terms.

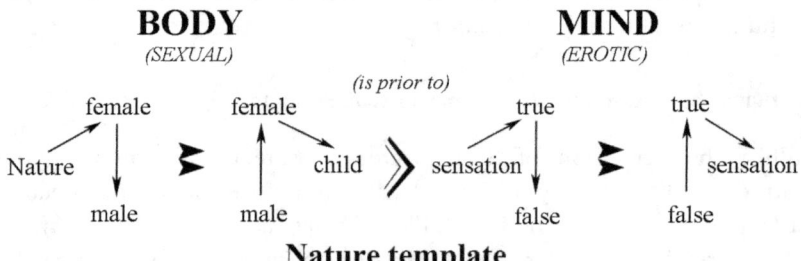

Nature template

To construct the *Nature template* we start with the relationship between the whole set as nature and the two sequences as female and male to create a *Female/male template* of the three givens to interrelate the priority of nature with the priority of the female over the male.

Then, taking the argument of the increase sonnets, we generate a similar configuration when the male recombines with the female to form a child in the *Male/female template*.

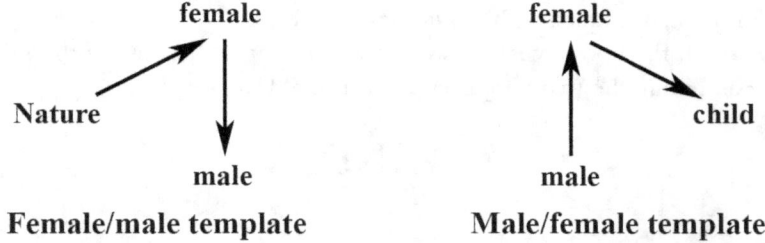

Female/male template **Male/female template**

We can then combine the two templates that represent the bodily or physical dynamic in nature to form the *Body template*. The left side of the template is biologically and hence logically prior to the right.

BODY
(SEXUAL)

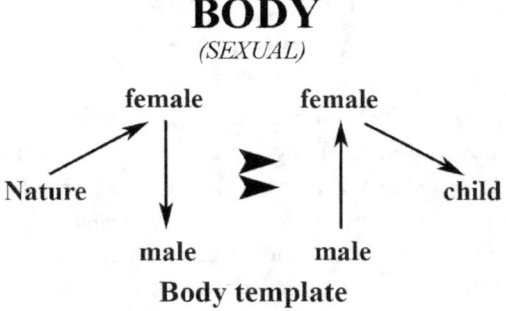

Body template

In the remaining 140 sonnets, the Poet argues for 'beauty' and 'truth' in the female sequence and for 'truth and beauty' in the male sequence. This means beauty and truth and truth and beauty are the characteristics of the mind immediately consequent on the body dynamic.

We can represent the logical relationship between them by using the

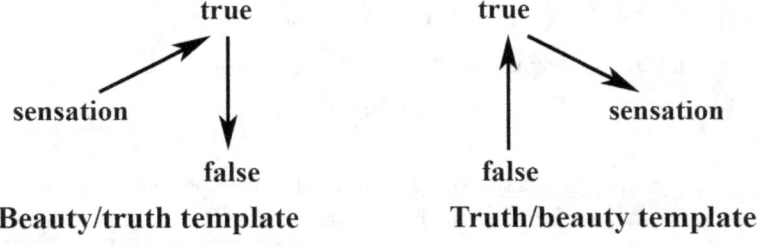

Beauty/truth template **Truth/beauty template**

word beauty to characterise singular sensations and truth to represent the polarity of language that typically allows the distinction between true and false. From the female sequence we have the *Beauty/truth template*, and from the male sequence the *Truth/beauty template*.

As with the body dynamic, we can represent the dynamic of the mind by combining the two templates to form the *Mind template*.

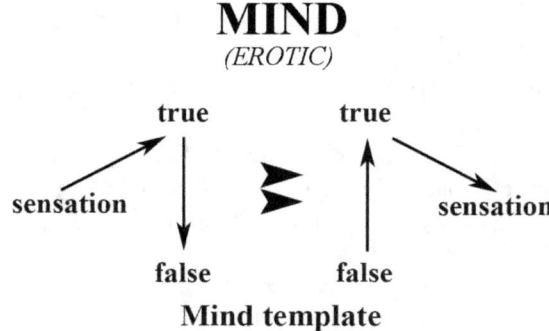

Mind template

In turn, the transitional sonnets *15* to *19* facilitate the relationship between the body and mind. They acknowledge the givens of nature, the female/male dynamic and the logic of increase cannot be argued for. When combining the *Body template* and *Mind template* to form a *Nature template* for the 154 sonnets, a double chevron indicates the role of the transitional sonnets *15* to *19*. Consequently, the *Body template* and the *Mind template* are isomorphic as the form of one develops out of the other.

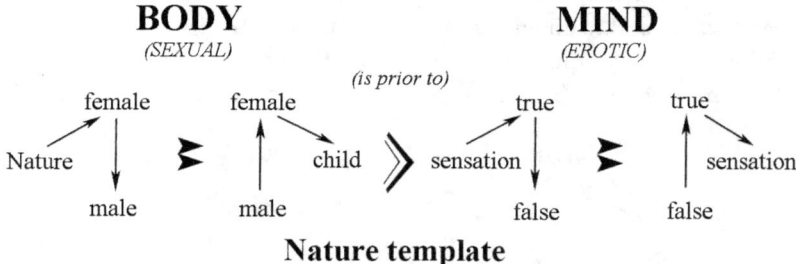

Nature template

By diagramming these logical inter-relationships, we represent the principal features of the set in the *Nature template*. The *Nature template* or map generates all the other possibilities in the set. Love (arising from physical or sensual beauty as well as from conceptual beauty or intuitions and emotions), music (as an expression of beauty synchronous with nature) and time (as a construct of language), all find their logical home in the *Nature template*. The *Nature template* gives graphic shape to the philosophy Shakespeare has in mind as he constructs all his poems and plays.

The complex of relationships in the set fall into place if the *templates* are kept mind while considering the two sequences, the interior groupings, the logically related sonnets and the individual sonnets. What was once difficult to penetrate is made comprehensible by bringing to bear upon the set its own self-organising logic.

Inverting the Nature template for male-based mind-based psychologies

By inverting the *Nature template* derived above from end-to-end, we can indicate the commentators' distance from Shakespeare's achievement. With brilliant irony Shakespeare's nature-based philosophy can be used to illustrate how the traditional biblical paradigm based on the mind-derived construct of a male God inverts the natural body/mind dynamic. We can approximate the inversion by swapping around the *Body* and *Mind* components of the *Nature template*, effectively making the map read backwards.

The resulting *God template*, shows how Shakespeare's nature-based *template* critiques biblical beliefs that prioritise a mind-derived sensation called God over nature.

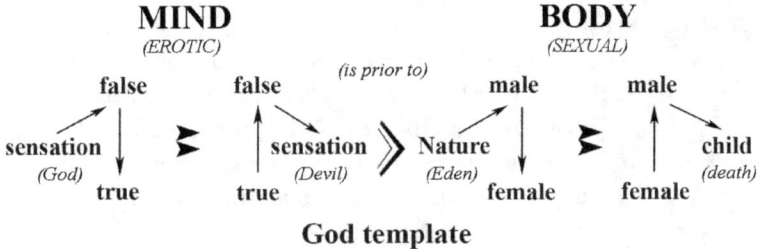

God template

All the contradictions of apologetics – deriving from justifying biblical conceits – follow from the illogical move of male usurpation of female priority. True and false lose their evolutionary rootedness in the female/male dynamic. The sensory world is branded evil and nature becomes idealised as Eden. The male usurps the priority of the female and childbirth becomes a sinful death sentence for disobedience to male-based conventions and impositions.

Shakespeare predicts that only when God-believers accept the limitations of their inverted paradigm will they recover their birthright natural philosophy. When they do, they will recognise the apparent obscurities and errors in Q and F are due to cataracts in their eyes and not to blotches on Shakespeare's page.

Applying the Nature template to understand and remedy typical scenarios

The first essay in this Volume, *How to Use the Nature Template*, considers a number of ways to apply the *Nature template* to resolve nine philosophical/psychological conundrums generated by the apologetic syndrome in Tertiary pedagogy. The conundrums arise when Tertiary attempts to account for or excuse inconsistencies and outright prejudices of the type represented by the *God template*.

The essay examines the typical Tertiary apologetic confusions about Philosophy and Psychology, Nature and God, Sexual and Erotic, Technocratic mindsets, Non-linear and Linear, Fact and Fiction, Sex and Gender. The essay concludes the analysis by itemising the many reverse psychological techniques Shakespeare uses to dissemble and remedy the above self-induced paroxysms.

Then follows an essay titled *From Male to Female: Where the Default Lies* that demonstrates the importance of accepting the originary status of the female common to all sexual species – including homo sapiens. The female-based status of all sexual species is particularly evident in the biological fact only the female of any sexual species from simple cellular organisms to sharks and lizards can self-replicate through parthenogenesis.

Moreover, all male-based myths acknowledge the default biological dynamic by offering pseudo replication through their constitutional eroticism. The acceptance of the natural female/male relationship would lead to greater peace and contentedness.

The essay titled *Shakespeare and Democracy* argues Shakespeare's nature-based female-validating philosophy is constitutionally democratic. Shakespeare's *Sonnet* philosophy, and particularly its application in the thirty-six plays in the 1623 *Folio*, counters and excoriates the patriarchal, autocratic misogynistic consequence of traditional male-based mind-based beliefs.

Then follows a group of four essays that consider the Quaternary implications of Shakespeare's nature-based philosophy for Tertiary academia and its history of apologetics. The *Creative University*, *Criteria for Quaternary*, *Quaternary Pedagogy*, and *Upgrading from Tertiary to Quaternary*, were written in response to issues raised by Tertiary academics.

Tertiary's inadequacy in its abject failure over the last 400 years to apprehend and understand Shakespeare's nature-based philosophy means only the institution of a Quaternary level of universal pedagogy can effectively supersede and obviate the Tertiary mind-set. Only a Quaternary level of understanding can provide an education for a Global constituency constantly conscious humans are a nature-based species despite them imagining otherwise.

Concluding remarks

Shakespeare's works have formed a significant part of the culture and curriculum over the preceding decades and centuries. His plays have been produced – albeit in bastardised forms – since they were written over four hundred years ago, his *Sonnets* have been read as the greatest love poems in the literature and his life has been celebrated and valourised.

However, it is only over the last fifty years that the predations of contrary productions and readings has begun to be addressed with gradual return to the original edition of the plays from 1623 and the *Sonnets* from 1609 to determine why the mangled editions have got it so wrong. Moreover, the trend now is not to produce ten or so plays wrongly considered the most Christian in the canon but all of the thirty-six plays from the *Folio* in tacit recognition that all of Shakespeare's works contain a philosophic and thematic consistency.

The discovery of the *Sonnet* philosophy in 1995 and the investigation of all his works in the light of the *Sonnet* philosophy – with subsequent publications – provides an opportunity to recognise the substantive basis of his poetic, dramatic and especially his philosophic achievement.

How to Use the Nature Template

CONTENTS

Preamble – Shakespeare's nature-based philosophy	3
Philosophy versus Psychology	10
Nature versus God	15
Sexual versus Erotic	19
Technocratic mind-sets	23
Christ the Carpenter	28
Non-linear and Linear	32
Fact versus Fiction	37
Sex versus Gender	41
Reverse Psychology	46
Conclusion	60

Preamble – Shakespeare's nature-based philosophy

The idea Shakespeare's deeply philosophic appreciation of the natural preconditions for life and art is both more consistent and comprehensive than that of any other recognised philosopher will strike some as contrary to the traditional view of Shakespeare as an incomparable 'Bard' with no intentional philosophy. After all, T. S. Eliot allows Shakespeare only a 'rag bag' philosophy at best, and William Wordsworth thinks the crucial twenty-eight Mistress sonnets a 'puzzle-peg'.

While many suspect there is a profound philosophy embedded in Shakespeare's works, they do not bring to the plays – and particularly the *Sonnets* – the appropriate degree of philosophical acuity or even common sense to appreciate readily Shakespeare's peerless achievement. However, it is not difficult to show Shakespeare structures his works – all his plays, sonnets and poems – with a completely consistent natural logic common to humankind within nature.

Once we apprehend and apply the required relationship of natural givens or preconditions, Shakespeare's *Folio* of thirty-six plays, his 154 sonnets and four longer poems suddenly become a brilliantly interrelated corpus of unmatched perspicacity and structural simplicity revealing the basis of the depth and breadth of his understanding and expression.

When Shakespeare arranges his *Sonnets* of 1609, he lays out systematically the natural dynamic of body and mind that informs all his poems and plays. The level of premeditated structuring is sufficient to derive the *Sonnet template* (below) as a schematic representation of his nature-based philosophy.

Shakespeare's *Sonnets* reveal a deliberate logical and numerological organisation into an overarching set of 154 sonnets that incorporates two sequences of 126 sonnets to the male and 28 sonnets to the female plus the increase argument of the first fourteen sonnets. Then follows the deliberate separation of beauty and truth in the Mistress sequence and conflation of truth and beauty in the Master Mistress sequence.

The representation of the thematic and numerical relationships in the *Sonnet template* show how the various parts of the 154-sonnet arrangement cohere isomorphically to provide a powerful tool for interpretation and exploration. The *Nature template - Sonnets* maintains the terminology of the 154-sonnet set to demonstrate how the 1609 *Sonnets* configure the relationships.

QUATERNARY ESSAYS: SHAKESPEARE'S NATURE-BASED PHILOSOPHY

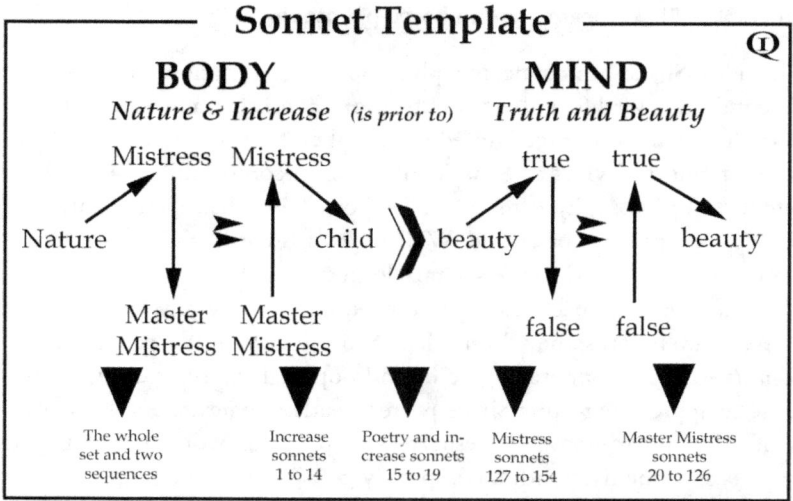

It is possible to reduce Shakespeare's semi-generic characterisation of the principal components of his philosophy in the 1609 *Sonnets* to their everyday equivalents to form a corresponding *Nature template*. The modifications identify Mistress as female, Master Mistress as male and beauty as sensation.

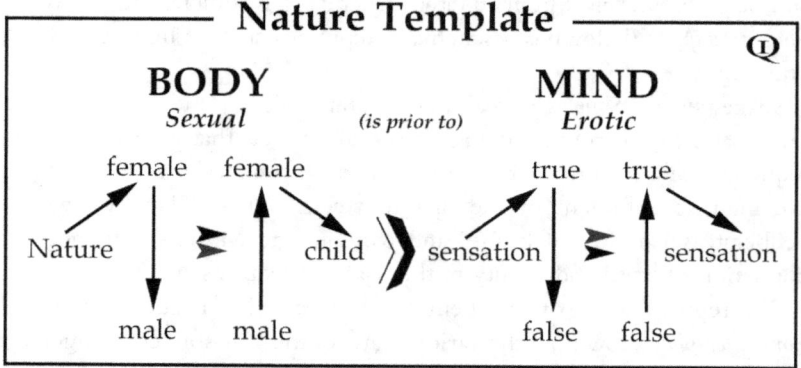

The everyday constituents of the *Nature template* show Shakespeare, more than any other thinker, includes only unquestionable givens or logical preconditions in the basic structuring of his *Sonnets* – as the basis for all his works. Each element is an irreducible feature of the constitution and operation of the human body and mind. They are not optional but essential components for the physical and cognitive functions of body and mind.

Shakespeare's philosophic tour de force both originates in and reconverges on the concept nature. Everything Shakespeare writes suggests he has an unerring appreciation that the word nature is the only overarching singularity in the English language (and in other Latinate languages), which is referred to entirely without qualification. In his *Sonnets* – and in his other works – the status of nature is never questioned but is accepted invariably as the ground from which all else entails.

The unique use of the word nature in everyday language reveals its logical status in the lexicon and grammar of thought, speech and writing. We use no other generic word – not universe, not world, not god – only in the singular. Similarly, no other word in English operates without articles such as 'the', 'an', or 'a', and nature does not have to resort to the faux singularity of a proper noun, as does the name God.

As Ludwig Wittgenstein realises, all words as vocalised sounds are effectively arbitrary before they are defined through their use in the language-game or grammar of language. Hence, the preference for the word nature to represent the singularity of everything not only preconfigures its uniqueness but also points to its logical ramifications within human life and thought.

The English word nature derives from the Latin natura ('birth', 'origin', etc.) or (g)natus ('born') or (g)nasci ('to be born', 'originate'). So the word chosen by apologetic philosophers such as Thomas Aquinas and Baruch Spinoza with which to characterise the relation between their monotheistic male God and 'His' creation carries with it the implication that nature and being born are etymologically inseparable.

Shakespeare recognises the fundamental link between nature at large and human procreation (again more consistently than any other thinker) when he structures his *Sonnet* set thematically and numerologically into two sexual sequences, one to the female and the other to the male – within the context of the whole set of 154 sonnets representing nature. Shakespeare dedicates twenty-eight sonnets to the female and 126 to the male, effectively dividing the set to replicate the sexual differentiation of male from female in nature.

Shakespeare's next move is entirely consistent with both nature's philosophic singularity and its archaic etymology. The precondition for any birth (human or other sexual species) in nature is the differentiation at some point in evolutionary/biological history of the male from the originary female with consequent requirement for the male to return to the female to perpetuate their kind.

It seems, then, Shakespeare's unprecedented inclusion of a female and male sequence in his set of 154 sonnets based in nature has a deeply biological/logical premise and consequence. That he understands this to be the case is confirmed when he has the first fourteen sonnets argue specifically for increase. They warn unequivocally of the irreversible outcome if all humans failed to increase (sonnet 11 specifically).

Already embedded in the word nature are the natural implications Shakespeare articulates in the overall structure of the set and the first set-piece argument for increase within the set. The sexual division of male from female in nature is not only the pivotal moment that leads to the multiplicity of human sexual and gender types and potentialities, its logical implications are pre-recorded in the word nature that grammatically represents our abiding sense of singularity.

With these three biological/logical moves, Shakespeare naturally – and so readily – constructs the first half of what we refer to as the *Nature template - Sonnets*. By logically aligning the preconditions for physical life, he effectively forms a completely consistent *Body template*. In turn, the *Body template* represents the natural precursors to the second half of the *Sonnet template*.

In the structural dynamic of Shakespeare's intensely philosophic 154 sonnets, his next move is to show how the logical operations of the human mind are configured entirely isomorphic with bodily dispositions. In keeping with the rigorous natural logic of his initial insights (configured within the *Body template*), the constituents of the *Mind template* consider only unarguable givens representing the human being's apprehensions, expressions and intuitions within singular nature.

Shakespeare begins his examination of human sensory perception by acknowledging every human being apprehends the natural world primarily through the senses. In the *Sonnets*, and particularly in the first eleven sonnets to the female (or Mistress), he uses the word 'beauty' to characterise the unprejudiced singularity of incoming sensations. He recognises (as do other philosophers) that the everyday sensations of colour, sound, smell, touch and taste are unbidden and unmediated singular effects (sonnets 127 to 137).

Then, as Shakespeare recognises in sonnets 138 to 152, the determination of true and false (a dynamic he calls 'truth') occurs only in the context of articulate language. In the grammar of language or saying, we continually swear and forswear concepts based in words to comprise the lexicon of possible or impossible conceptual correspondences to things in nature.

Lastly are the interior sensations of the mind (that Shakespeare also calls beauty) such as intuitions and visions that occur initially as singular unbidden and unmediated effects arising from the unconscious mind. Such sensations are then either articulated in language or given singular expression in music, poetry or art. Shakespeare dedicates the lengthy sequence to the male or Master Mistress to discussing the natural logic and ramifications of mind-derived sensations (sonnets 20 to 126).

Shakespeare's *Sonnets* recognise that these three organically dynamic activities – incoming sensations, enlanguaged ideas of right and wrong, and interior sensations of the mind – are the logical basis for all sensory, cognitive and imaginative possibilities. They constitute the irreducible components of the second half of the *Sonnet template* or the *Mind template*.

The layout of the complete *Nature template* makes visible the derivation of mind-based activities in the *Mind template* from their isomorphic precursors in the *Body template*. In evolutionary or Darwinian terms, it is not surprising that the *Mind template* should morph out of the *Body template* as the mind derives from the body over evolutionary time.

Shakespeare acknowledges the body to mind development by recognising that logically anything he says about the *Body template* presumes on the reflectivity and reflexivity of the *Mind template*. In other words, he accepts that what he says and writes about nature and the sexual dynamic has only as much soundness as his mind's ability to remain completely at one with his body's natural dispositions and logical alignment.

Shakespeare dedicates five sonnets (15 to 19) immediately after the fourteen increase sonnets to facilitate the transition from the sexual dynamic in nature to its natural correlate in the sensory and cognitive functions of the human mind. He accepts the *Mind template* derives from the *Body template* and conversely everything he thinks, says or writes depends on the body dynamic for its perspicacity and potentiality.

One of the consequences of aligning the natural givens from the *Sonnets* in the *Nature template* to form the *Body template* and the *Mind template* is a graphic insight into Shakespeare's appreciation of the logical distinction between the sexual and the erotic. In his *Sonnets*, there is a clear separation of the literal arguments about the significance of the sexual dynamic from the more evocative or even provocative verse as he moves to make the erotic dynamic palpable for the protagonists.

Shakespeare very deliberately identifies the sexual with the female/male differentiation in nature and the consequent requirement for increase. Similarly, he is equally determined in identifying the erotic with all mind-based constructs and their attendant desires while recognising the erotic is logically consequent on the sexual dynamic in nature.

Shakespeare appreciates that the most overdetermined mind-based construct, the biblical monotheistic God, demonstrates through His purely erotic genesis (as with the plethora of Goddesses and Gods in creation myths) that all mind-based activities are inherently erotic because they are imaginative constructs founded logically on the sexual dynamic in nature.

This very brief summary of the derivation of the *Nature template* from *Shakespeares Sonnets* of 1609 and the intimation he publishes the 154-sonnet set to present the philosophy behind all his plays and poems is based on the evidence and argument available at length and in detail in published volumes (2005 and forthcoming) and on the Quaternary Institute website.

Crucial to the purposes of the current essay is the simple demonstration the *Sonnet template* both conforms to evident structural features of the 1609 *Sonnets* and is logically sound. It supersedes all attempts over 4000 years by more psychologically afflicted philosophers to develop a sound philosophy free from the need to validify speculative claims for any mind-based constructs - particularly the biblical God, who usually gets a get out of jail free card by apologists.

As we consider a number of philosophic issues in the following sections of this essay, it will become apparent traditional apologetic reformulations of the sound logic of the *Nature template* that attempt to represent the claims of biblical religions for their mind-based male-based God and his pantheon of mind-based constructs reveal the illogicality and hubris associated with such supererogatory constructions.

The *God template* (below) is merely the worst-case scenario that characterises (inevitably crudely) the intractability of mind-based male-based beliefs. It shows clearly why such beliefs are at odds with nature and the natural implications for human physical and mental well-being.

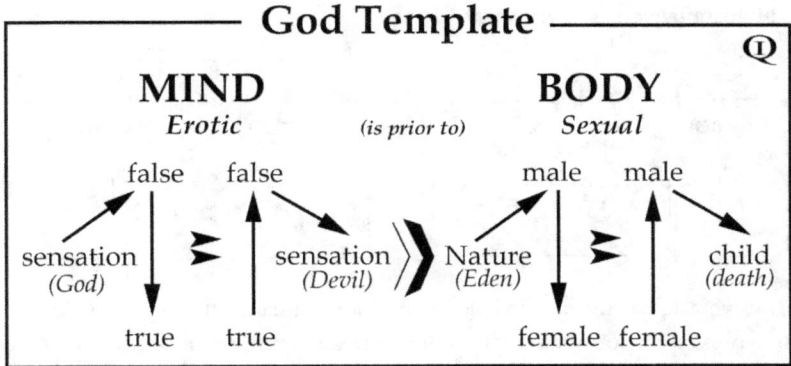

The intent in the following sections of the essay is to take a number of seemingly disparate issues and show how to apply the *Nature template* to first analyse the problematic situations and then either facilitate their resolution or demonstrate the reason for their intractability. We will see that conformity to the *Nature template* allows philosophic perspicacity whereas distortions to the *Nature template* to form equivalents of the *God template* prevent such consistency and comprehensiveness.

1) Philosophy versus Psychology

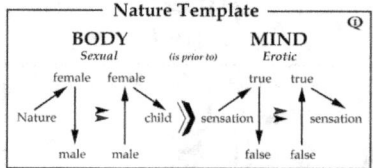 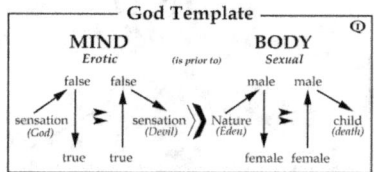

Why, we ask, has no one in 400 years since William Shakespeare's death in 1616 previously sounded out his consistent and comprehensive nature-based *Sonnet* philosophy? Moreover, as a corollary, what has traditional or academic philosophy been doing over the last 400 years or more if it has not been doing philosophy?

The simple answer is that all other philosophers over the last few millennia have been in varying degrees practicing psychology in the guise of philosophy. Consequently, not one 'great' – or lesser – philosopher from the 1600s onwards appreciates the profound and systematic philosophy in Shakespeare's works.

In contrast, because Shakespeare bases his understanding in a sound and encompassing nature-based philosophy, he has deeply penetrating insights into the near universally practiced psychology-as-philosophy syndrome. His nature-based philosophy also enables him to give unprecedented expression to the vicissitudes of human psychology (including the idea of an imaginary soul) throughout his play and poems.

Even modern nature-orientated thinkers prove blind to the sound and comprehensive nature-based philosophy in Shakespeare's *Sonnets*. Their shortcomings relate directly to the role many have as academics in Tertiary philosophy departments – or an undue faith in such academics.

Effectively, most so-called philosophers are still constrained by the fact Universities were founded around 1100AD with the express expectation scholars would justify the biblical belief in an omnipotent Creator God. Consequently, apologetics has been the principal form of philosophic practice over the last 400 years – and the vestiges of its justificatory techniques continue to afflict even the most skeptical thinkers.

Furthermore, all apologetic thinkers before 1100AD were similarly determined to demonstrate the cogency of male-based biblical beliefs through the process of valid rather than sound argument. However, because all such beliefs are mind-based constructs or mind-induced desires, then the corresponding so-called philosophy amounts to no more than psychological justification for reified or personified imaginary ideals and expectations.

Once a mind-based construct like the biblical monotheistic God is given priority over nature and is enforced as dogma, it inverts the natural order of body before mind. When believers make the mind prior to the body, and in effect subsume the body into its mind-based creativity, inconsistencies abound not the least of which is the perennial – and ironically named – mind/body problem.

That many so-called philosophers address themselves to the mind/body problem over the centuries without questioning the psychological perversion the inversion of the body/mind dynamic represents indicts their faith in the redemptive value of valid argumentative ploys – which early logicians including Aristotle invent wittingly or unwittingly for them.

Comparing the *Nature template*'s sound natural logic with the contrived logical validity of the *God template* makes graphic the artificiality of the mind/body problem. The only justification for persisting with the rampant inconsistencies of the *God template* is the psychological vulnerability – or sometimes bravado – of those at dispositional odds with their natural body/mind trajectory.

What sets Shakespeare apart from every apologetic philosopher is the comprehensiveness of his nature-based understanding that incorporates the female/male priority (anathema to male-based beliefs) consistently all the way to the deepest sensations and soulful intuitions of the imaginative mind. By doing so, he demonstrates the complete illogicality of the *God template* with its pretentious occlusion of the originary female and the preemptive substitution of a purely mind-based sensation of psychological singularity and simplicity (hubristically named God) for the incontestability of the philosophic unity and diversity of nature.

While no other thinker has Shakespeare's depth and range, in the early Twentieth Century the philosopher Ludwig Wittgenstein does set out to reject imposed metaphysical imperatives and recover a sound philosophy from the mess of historical psychological speculation. After attempting – but failing definitively – in his first period of work to show language is reducible to an atomic/molecular logic derived from nuclear physics, Wittgenstein subsequently makes tentative moves towards a more broadly nature-based understanding.

Returning to philosophy in the 1930s, Wittgenstein begins by demonstrating that language generates meaning only through the natural dynamic of everyday use over time. He comes to appreciate that 'language games' are founded on 'forms of life' and the facts of 'nature' and having 'parents' and these natural givens provide the unquestionable basis of 'certainty' for the purposeful function of any language game.

In the later years of his career, Wittgenstein also writes at length on the philosophy of psychology. His treatment of the philosophical/psychological confusion, though, only goes as far as psychological phenomena such as visual illusions. His investigation focuses on the phenomenon he calls 'seeing as'. Typically, 'seeing as' involves the ability of the mind to see two different images in the same shape but not at the same time – as in the often reproduced duck/rabbit diagram.

Underlying Wittgenstein's investigations into the philosophy of psychology is the deeper issue of mistaking psychology for philosophy. Unfortunately, while Wittgenstein does appreciate that nature and parents are unquestionable givens in regard to mind-based activity, he does not devise a systematic account of the relationship between natural philosophic certainties and visual psychological conundrums.

While Wittgenstein does identify nature and parents as unquestionable givens, in the context of his simplistic take on the philosophy of psychology, other thinkers ignore his natural grounds for language and focus on the apparent relativistic implications of his examination of sensory conundrums. What certainty, they ask, can philosophy have if simple visual phenomena lead to conflicting interpretations? Hence, the ease with which such thinkers align Wittgenstein with psychological philosophies such as post-modernism.

The confusions arise and multiply because those practicing psychology as if they are doing philosophy cannot see past the mind-based constructs psychology generates. From their mind-based disadvantage, they consider both philosophy and psychology to be irredeemably rooted in the mind and hence both subject to the same doubts and historicity.

Both mind-based/mind-based beliefs and modern skepticism – typified by the post-modern malaise – consider the mind prior to the body. Effectively, they lock themselves into a self-validating trance that denigrates the body – and hence nature.

Over three-hundred years before Wittgenstein provides a mere sketch of the relation between philosophy and psychology, Shakespeare adroitly and profoundly redresses the philosophic issues Wittgenstein tentatively investigates in his determination to find certainty beyond traditional mind/based metaphysics. Shakespeare does so by first recovering the natural logic of human evolution of body before mind and structures his philosophy with only unquestionable givens. By accepting uncontestable preconditions, he then shows how and where psychology relates to philosophy.

The confusion in conflating psychology and philosophy evaporates by recognising philosophy as the relationship between the unarguable givens or natural preconditions for both the human body and mind. Shakespeare is the only philosopher who sets out all the natural givens basic to human existence and consequently for the operations of the human mind. He is also a peerless poet and playwright who is able to give vivid expression to his insights into everyday human life and the depths of mature love.

Each of the components of the *Nature template* is unequivocal and irreplaceable for human beings to be the sort of thinking and emotional animals they are. From singular nature, to the sexual dynamic of female and male and the logic of increase devolves the constitutional sensory, language and super sensory faculties of the mind. The fact of human sexuality in nature and the consequent isomorphic capacity of the mind to use language to interrelate true and false amidst sensory inputs and outputs underpin all other possibilities.

Whereas philosophy sets out the natural relation between body and mind in terms of unarguable givens, psychology pertains only to the operations of the mind as it responds to opportunities and vicissitudes in the world. The syndrome of confounding philosophy with psychology arises in part because the body dynamic of sexual increase in nature is the precondition for the operations of the mind. This ironically leads to the reflexive ability of the mind to reconstitute the natural dynamic within its own parameters creating the illusion of an organisation independent of nature – typically the *God template* of biblical religions.

The single most revealing marker of such inversions of natural philosophy is the eroticism underlying all myths of origins. The confusion of sexuality with eroticism and vice versa in modern psychology and psychiatry has its roots in the unwillingness to address fully the inversions introduced by male-based faiths a few thousand years ago.

Shakespeare's perennial influence both on philosophy and psychology, with philosophers writing books attempting to explain the philosophic depth in Shakespeare's works and psychiatrists misattributing his characters' traits onto Shakespeare himself, belies his unparalleled clarity about the logical relation of philosophy and psychology. By comparison, Wittgenstein flounders in the simplistic sensory implications of the conundrum.

The *Nature template* (readily derivable from the *Sonnets*) shows incontrovertibly just how philosophy, psychology, the sexual and the erotic, body and mind stand in relation to one another.

2) Nature versus God

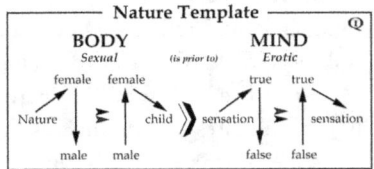
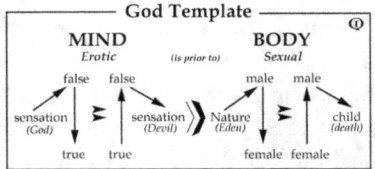

Apologetic philosophers from Thomas Aquinas (1225-74), Baruch Spinoza (1632-77) and Friedrich Nietzsche (1844-1900) – and even contemporary thinkers – perennially attempt to reconcile the issues of ascendancy surrounding the words God and nature. With the recovery of Greek thought in the early Renaissance, the conflict between Plato and Aristotle – between absolute idealism and natural empiricism – resurfaces in the standoff over God and nature.

It is no accident of etymology or epistemology that such philosophers swing the debate around the two words God and nature. The monotheistic God of the Bible, as the most singular of the religiously unborn, represents all mind-derived entities not generated through the natural process of procreation (or as Shakespeare calls it – increase). The word nature on the other hand derives from the Latin natura (natus) or nasci meaning to be born. Hence, nature represents everything that depends on or subtends upon the dynamic of increase.

The mono-God, then, represents effectively all mind-based male-based constructs and anything not subject to the natural dynamic of increase. Specifically, because there are no correlates to mind-derived sensations external to the human mind, the idea of God is a purely mind-based fabrication or fantasy.

In contrast, nature represents everything that devolves around the natural propensity to propagate and the necessity to procreate for the persistence of sexual species. If humankind, for instance, decides not to procreate – or neglects to do so en masse – there will be no more believers to sustain the mind-based sensation called God, but the full panoply of nature (sans humans) would continue regardless.

The response of philosophers to the God/nature question is as diverse as Aquinas' attempting to show God commands nature, to Spinoza arguing God and nature represent the same thing – or to Nietzsche announcing the death of God. Then there are modern philosophers who argue the mind is dependent on the body and so any mind-based constructs like God are logically dependent on nature – and not vice versa.

Yet it is William Shakespeare who systematically and effectively corrects all the traditional anomalies – and the subsequent apologetic posturing. Implicit in his organisation of the 1609 *Sonnets* (as the basis for all his plays) is a nature-based philosophy that logically differentiates and delineates the meanings of the words nature and God. Shakespeare's clarity about the exact relationship is both unparalleled and comprehensive of the breadths and depths of the relationship.

The structural arrangement of the 154 sonnets – which the *Nature template* represents – shows the logical priority of the basic components with singular nature as the groundedness for the eventual manifestation of the interior sensation of the mind believers call God.

By ascribing 154 sonnets to nature, Shakespeare recognises the unique grammar of the word nature, which occurs only in the singular when referring to nature at large. By giving nature the numbering 154, Shakespeare knows that traditional numerological addition configures its unity: $154 = 1+5+4 = 10 = 1+0 = 1$. Similarly, in English, the word nature uniquely accepts no articles such as the, an or a – as do the words God, universe, world, etc.

The distinctive grammar of the two words nature and God should be sufficient to show that ever-present nature is the logically singular default or given and the sensation called God (or whatever name) is a mind-based language-dependent construct subtending on the naturally evolved body/mind dynamic. Furthermore, the word God cribs its apparent singularity as a name by capitalising on the conventional uniqueness of proper nouns.

While Shakespeare appreciates the simplicity of the demonstration, he knows there are contributing factors militating against an easy acceptance of the obvious. Over the last 4000 or so years, each of the principal components of the *Nature template* has been subject to dislocation or even complete inversion as a consequence of the beguiling influence of believing the mind-generated sensation called God has priority over all else – and bizarrely creates everything out of nothing

Typically, biblical mythology idealises nature as an Edenic Paradise and elevates the male as precursor for the female. In biblical myth, the female becomes the locus of death rather than physical increase, whereas in nature the female and not the male is the locus of the birth process. With their immaculate conceptions, virgin births, disembodied resurrections and re-embodied judgments, death is the perpetual recourse of such religions.

In turn, the biblical about-face brands immediate sensations as the source of evil rather than unmediated or neutral inputs to the mind. The upshot is to invert the natural true/false dynamic, with mind-based constructs (like the male God) given priority over natural contingencies. Ironically, biblical devotees worship interior sensations of the mind as fully cognizant and literary, rational Gods and Goddesses.

Basic to the perverted religious syndrome is the inclination to prioritise the mind over the body. Consequent on the seductive attractivity of mind-based sensations is the confusion of the eroticism of mind-based desires for body-determined sexuality. All Gods and Goddesses, including the monotheistic God of the Bible, are born of erotic and not sexual processes.

The *Nature template* captures with incredible economy the verifiable dynamic and identifies precisely those elements so readily distorted by mind-based beliefs. In the *Sonnets*, Shakespeare discusses the various elements and their susceptibility to corruption by mind-based zealotry.

It is possible to represent the distortions in the *God template* (illustrated in the preamble) that inverts the *Nature template* to show the corruptions and their consequences. The *Nature template*, in the light of the corrupt *God template*, critiques the faulty logic behind the inclination to invert, confuse or conflate the relationship between the word God and nature. Nature is the uniquely singular word that encapsulates all else including the singular mind-based sensation named God.

The word nature represents all possibilities by default – not by convention or legislation. In contrast, the word God while also referring to singular sensations of the mind – even the most intense sensations of connectivity and purposefulness – requires special etymological conditions to represent that singularity. It acquires a capital G and the first three Mosaic Commandments to regulate it into its privileged position by capitalising on the singular reference of proper nouns. Whereas no other word readily substitutes for nature, God has synonyms in Allah, Jehovah, et al., – all with capitals and all imposed by fiat.

Shakespeare recognises that the *God template* inverts wholesale the *Nature template*. He not only clearly details the type and extent of the corruption, he also examines in the thirty-six *Folio* plays the malconsequences and gratuitous violence that follow when believers in whatever version of the *God template* ignore their common base in nature and impose and enforce their mind-based/male based beliefs.

While Shakespeare acknowledges in detail the inversion of natural logic into cul-de-sacs of psychological intractability, he is also uses methods throughout his works to reverse psychologise the impasses and cruelty issuing from the imposition of the *God template* as a universal norm. He uses a variety of tactics to counter the worst consequences of its unbridled application.

(See Section 9 for a discussion of Shakespeare's reverse psychological methods.)

3) Sexual versus Erotic

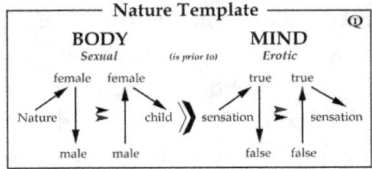 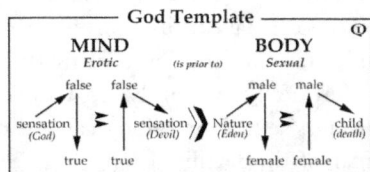

The most perversely erotic entity the human imagination ever creates is the male-based mind-based monotheistic God of biblical myth. More sensationally erotic than pornographic imagery or even nudity in religious art, the singular sensation called God both genuinely evokes and simultaneously misrepresents the deepest erotic impulses in the human mind.

The apparently self-creating mono-God of revealed religion not only capitalises on the deepest mind-based sensations, in biblical myth scribes intensify the mind-generated pure erotic frisson by declaring 'His' priority over the originary female and the biology of increase – so effectively the whole of nature.

When ancient scribal cultures were established, male-orientated myths of origins provide the overarching contexts under which Kings and Queens rule – and still rule – with impunity. Even in Twenty-first Century democracies, the biblical myth remains entrenched in the Anglicanism and Monarchy of Great Britain and hence the British Commonwealth.

Similarly, in republics like the United States of America, despite the separation of State and Church in the American Constitution, Christianity resurfaces by default in State functions and institutions. Of the growing number of democracies in the world, many still pay obeisance in their political observances to the God of the undemocratic and misogynistic churches.

Significantly, in the global demography, the multiplicity of myths in a plethora of world religions reveals the inherent factionalism behind traditional male-based beliefs. As a consequence, in the absence of a viable global myth, there is a burgeoning awareness of the natural logic that enables mythic expression.

Significantly, the French artist Marcel Duchamp (1887-1966) provides an exacting critique of the conditions for mythic expression in his *Bride*

Stripped Bare by Her Bachelors, Even (1912-23) and Étant donnés (1946-68). Moreover, 300 years earlier Shakespeare gives an even more trenchant critique of the logic of myth in his 1609 *Sonnets* and 1623 *Folio* of plays.

The crucial distinction both Duchamp and Shakespeare make for understanding the logic of mythic expression is between the sexual and the erotic. Significantly, no Goddess or God in mythical stories is born through sexual or biological means – i.e. through the womb and birth canal of the fertilised female. The non-sexual genesis of all inaugurating Goddesses and/or Gods from the multitude of world religions signals that all mind-based sensations are inherently or logically erotic – as are the language constructs they inspire.

The *Nature template* highlights the natural logic of the sexual-to-erotic dynamic basic to all living beings, which Shakespeare articulates in full in his *Sonnets* and explores in his plays. Conversely, the *God template* clearly shows the inversion of the dynamic when it institutes the erotic as the precursor for the sexual. The inconsistencies and injustices consequent on the willful corruption of the *Nature template* speak to the philosophic illogicalities and gratuitous injustices endemic to all male-based mind-based beliefs.

The myths of origin at the heart of the world's cultures memorialise the mind-based birth suite of all goddesses and gods in societies' religions. For devotees, the inscribed eroticism underscoring the representations of their goddesses and gods in myths manufactures the attractivity of religious texts.

In other words, by swallowing the body dynamic whole into the mind dynamic, biblical myth converts nature into a vast paradisiacal erotic landscape (the most recent manifestation of which is the metaphysical theory of the Big Bang). Ungoverned by natural prerogatives, the God of biblical myth – in a glowing personification that leaves His more salacious counterparts from the realm of mind-satiating artistry in the shade – evinces the most idealistically pure mind-enhanced epiphanies. However, exactly the same deeply felt sensations when called God can incite equally intense mind-based delusions leading to the most gratuitous of murderous excesses.

Crucially, Shakespeare recognises that the unacknowledged deep eroticism at the heart of biblical religions, while satiating the mythic potentialities of the human mind, inverts and distorts the natural relationship between the sexual body and the erotic mind. The combination of satiated mind-based sensations and the elevation of their deeply affective singularities to venerated divinities speaks to the intensity of the sensations but also to an ignorance of their natural mind-alone provenance and religious inversion.

Gian Lorenzo Bernini captures brilliantly – if somewhat unintentionally – the relationship between the divine and the erotic in his rapturous sculpture *The Ecstasy of Saint Teresa* (~1650). In his exquisite marble evocation of the ecstatic moment Carmelite Teresa of Avila consummates her heady union with God, Bernini interprets her notes as suggesting she simultaneously masturbates to an erotic climax.

Ironically, the Catholic Church's general proscription on masturbation foists unfairly on the laity a measure required to discourage the onanism rife amongst an unnaturally eroticised celibate clergy. The paedophilia prevalent amongst religious orders is a criminal consequence of the consecrated puerility of hermetic eroticism.

The *Nature template* illustrates clearly the source of the delusion as well as the reason for its mind-altering intensity and apparent intractability. Because everything, including the mind-based sensation called God, is part of nature, then at the deepest levels in the human mind the sensations experienced are effectively the mind's simulacrum of its connectedness to the whole of nature.

No wonder the experience of the deeply erotic sensation called God has the capacity to lull the mind into preferring a delimited version of nature pseudo-certified free of the perceived vicissitudes of the sexual dynamic. The Churches and their avatars like Jesus Christ – whose erotic death on the Cross forges a promissory guarantee or I.O.U. for asexual bliss in eternity – proffer an anodyne Heaven.

Shakespeare's plays and longer poems explore and critique the full gamut of the dubious legacy of the mind-marooned biblical God – and Christ – but always from within the context of the natural logic of the nature-based philosophy articulated in the *Sonnets* of 1609. Shakespeare covers the range from the rarified closet eroticism in monasteries and nunneries to their unbridled counterpart, the murderous machinations of King Richard III. *Richard III* evokes 'God' one hundred times – significantly more mentions of the word God than in of any Shakespeare's other Comedies, Histories and Tragedies in the 1623 *Folio*.

When biblical and other idealising mythologies corrupt the *Nature template* to form the inverted equivalent effectively as the *God template*, they render the sexual secondary to the erotic. Because the female is the precursor for the male in nature, the inversion creates a syndrome in which the female needs to be continuously denigrated and marginalized.

Hence, the Churches through their predominantly male-exclusive hierarchies proscribe both increase and sexuality. The consequence is the obscenity of a male clergy imposing unnatural strictures on childbirth and delimiting the natural multiplicity of gender dispositions to a unequal duality of dominant male and subservient female.

The impositions of beliefs in mind-based Gods who logically cannot procreate is completely at odds with a woman's natural right to manage her body and hence her pregnancy – through abortion if necessary. Moreover, the similar disregard for the natural formation of a variety of feminine and masculine gender types such as homosexuals, transsexuals, lesbians, etc., in the period after conception reveals the illogicality of enforcing the belief in male supremacy constitutional to male-based mythologies.

The iniquities are particularly acute in Churches like the Catholic where the Pope is staunchly celibate and monks and nuns become role models for all believers – in imitation of a Christ crucified without progeny. Hence, the Catholic Church is most extreme in enforcing unnatural practices and expectations on its adherents under threat of excommunication.

The terrible irony – maybe even the elusive reverse psychology of Shakespearean irony – is that a Church that outlaws abortions and homosexuals is itself the most diabolically erotic entity ever instituted – worse than explicit pornography or even whorehouses. At least those practices, in which increase remains a possibility, do not sanctify the celibate eroticism personified in the anti-nature, anti-female and anti-sexual figurehead of Papal righteousness.

4) Technocratic mind-sets

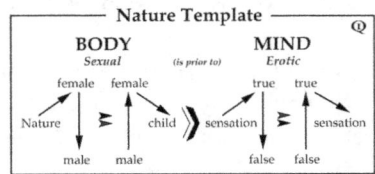 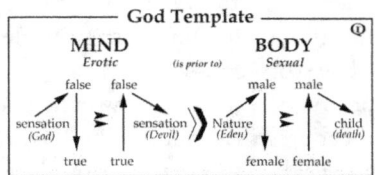

In the minds of those with deeply ingrained linear or technocratic dispositions or tendencies, a belief in overly imaginative constructs such as creation myths, cosmological constants, imminent robotics, the ascendancy of artificial intelligence, or even Big Bangs, can override or completely confound the natural relationships evident in the *Nature template*.

An insight into the source of the syndrome emerges by following the *Nature template* through from one end to the other. It is then possible to throw light on the reasons why those with technocratic or linear mind-sets have difficulty moderating their fascination with mind-based inventions and fantasies.

Thinkers and/or practitioners with technocratic dispositions frequently minimize or dismiss the first or *Body* half of the *Nature template*. They focus instead on localised areas of the second or *Mind* half of the *Nature template* – the investigative fact-to-facture (or true/false) dynamic of language and the imaginative facility driven by interior sensations in the mind.

Such thinkers ignore or denigrate the first half of the *Nature template* – with its uncontestable givens – in their headlong desire to ordain and exploit mind-based inventiveness and creativity. They overlook or dismiss the universality and singularity of nature, the undeniability of female priority and the logic of increase in their beguilement with and advocacy for purely mind-based constructs.

Ironically, the mind's ability to generate and accommodate an extraordinary number of facts and fictions is isomorphic with the body's capacity to generate billions of similar but non-identical human beings – along with its untapped reservoir of multi-cellular potential. The mind both accommodates a multitude of facts and conceptualises a vast array of imaginative possibilities of which only a fraction are practical enough to be manufactured into items useful for human productivity and survival.

While there may be a number of biological or conceptual mechanisms driving the tendency to prioritise mind-based constructs, once embedded in susceptible minds – and the syndrome can be apparent in either males or females – the inclination to believe in technocratic solutions without reflection seems almost irreversible.

The worst consequences of the near religious belief in such over-reaching constructs can be constrained only by constitutional or legislative procedures that enforce the birthright sensibility of the complete *Nature template*. Foremost is the American Constitution where Thomas Jefferson (in particular) appreciates the logic of instituting the total separation of a nature-based State from a male-God based Church. The Constitution prevents any of the many religious constructs from becoming the religion of the United States or of individual States.

The need to enact precautionary legislative measures to counter linear technocratically inspired beliefs and impositions anticipates the religious fervor with which over-masculinised minds invert the natural body/mind relationship. Such minds override the isomorphic connectivity between the originary female and offshoot male and the consequent capacity of the mind to mirror the biological relationship in the language dynamic that arbitrates the logic of true and false.

When viewed in the light of the *Nature template* derived from Shakespeare's works, the connection between body-based givens that generate the offshoot male (who depends on the female for reproductivity) and mind-based constructs (that appear to stand apart from nature) is plain to see.

The isomorphic relationships across the *Body/Mind* connectivity of the *Nature template* make it possible to appreciate the logical consequences the singularity of the originary female and the provisional status of the offshoot male have for the language dynamic of true and false. The female corresponds to 'true' because within sexual species she is the undifferentiated groundedness for all human possibilities while the male corresponds to 'false' because in the larger evolutionary process the female can survive without his sexual contribution.

As Shakespeare argues in the *Sonnets*, the archetypal recalcitrant male is fated to die 'alone' if he (and hence the whole of humankind) ignores the logic of increase. Likewise ideas developed in language out of the imagination (the 'false' in the *Mind* half of the *Nature template*) lose their connectivity to nature if they are treated as self-actuating and/or self-perpetuating entities.

The manic tendency to act against the natural prerogative to increase, further exacerbates the irrecoverability from immersion in the seductiveness of mind-based constructs. Biologically the male cannot exist independent of the female and also expect to persist across generations.

Unconditional religious celibacy, for instance, is a self-defeating syndrome that requires generation after generation of sexual propagated males to commit to the erotic celibate fantasy. Every God-infallible Pope is born of a biological mother – and father.

The delusional syndrome of male-alone perpetuation has its source in the biology of sexual reproduction where some originary female embryos become more masculinised and correspondingly are proportionately less feminised. After conception, in the process of cell division and with the feminisation and masculinisation of the zygote, there are varying degrees to which genes and hormones engender the balance of masculinisation in relation to the underpinning feminization.

For those males who are born more masculinised than feminised (and similarly for overly masculinised females) there appears to be a collateral tendency to accept – or believe religiously in – the 'false' part of the true/false dynamic in human understanding through language and sensations. Even more so, is the susceptibility to male-based mind-based constructs that are no more than reified manifestations of inner sensation of the human mind.

The most difficult constructs to ameliorate are those that verbalise, configure or give form to pure male-based/mind-based sensations – typically, the deepest singular sensation is called God, or other equally evocative epithets. Such pure mind-based constructs – originally generated speculatively for enhancing the deeper cultural intimations and expressivity of the species – when divorced from their sexual and sensory basis in nature become blindly exclusive, frequently exploitative and often destructive.

To some, the interrelationship of the isomorphic components of the *Nature template*, with the base physicality of the body dynamic and the consequent conceptuality of the mind dynamic, appear enigmatically random yet at the same time seem inexplicably determined. Not surprisingly, the apparent conflict is incomprehensible when viewed from the engineered logic of biblical prerogatives with their male-based prejudices and expectations.

The irony intensifies because the types of structure instituted by technocrats are extremely linear mind-based inventions that lack the flexibility and resiliency of the natural structure of the *Nature template*. While there is a full spectrum of sensibilities evident in human potentiality from non-linear to linear, the narrowed focus of the technocratic mindset leads to a prioritizing of minutiae and infinities over more grounded natural implications and possibilities.

For those disposed toward conceptual linear processes, mind-devised regularities such as scientific laws, digital systems (versus analog), mathematical constants (such as equality, zero and infinity) and their applications have a seductive certainty and universality. Yet the invention of all the computing constructs is datable to identifiable moments in recent history before which only the certainty and regularity of nature prevails.

One of the worst consequences of the technocratic mindset is the imposition of linear social, political and religious constructs on the thoughts and writings of thinkers like Charles Darwin, Marcel Duchamp, and Ludwig Wittgenstein. Wittgenstein appreciates the irony when he comments that if mathematicians listened to his critique of their methods and expectations it might be the worse day for mathematics. In his wisdom, he accepts that an unfettered technocratic mind-set is necessary to ensure continual inventiveness.

The thinker linearly addicted tertiary scholars most grievously afflict and disrespect, though, is William Shakespeare. They alter his texts to conform with their linear religious beliefs or reattribute significant parts of his works to other writers of decidedly linear dispositions – dispositions that are ironically closer to their own limited tertiary sensibilities and expectations.

Unable to accept or accommodate Shakespeare's unmatched ability to give expression to both non-linear and linear syndromes, such scholars do not reflect on their own limited technocratic sensibilities. Instead, they use their hubristic status in the publishing world to cover-up and perpetrate deceptions that rate as the most heinous literary crimes foisted on a literary giant.

Shakespeare examines the syndrome in great detail in his *Folio* of thirty-six plays. In the Comedies, he shows how to ameliorate the worst effects of male-based/mind-based impositions and, in the Histories and Tragedies, he presents twenty-two case studies of the unalloyed application of such constructs in fomenting societal mayhem and murderous intrigue.

Twenty years after beginning to write plays around 1590, Shakespeare publishes the 154 sonnets in 1609 to provide a consistent and comprehensive natural logic for the analysis and resolution of such mind-based disasters and cruelty. That it has taken 400 years for the *Sonnet* logic to be recognised points to the degree to which God-like technocratic expectations are inured in the culture.

5) Christ the Carpenter

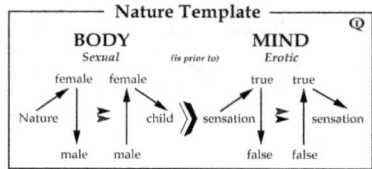
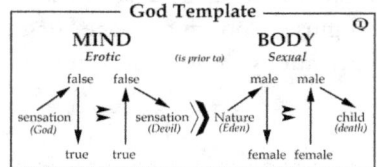

A common refrain from churchgoers and particularly their clergy when fires, earthquakes or floods damage or destroy their consecrated buildings is that, after all, God's love and the Church is really in the people themselves. The implication is that ecclesiastic structures are secondary or incidental to a belief in God – that God exists independently of visible structures built by humans, because the constructions merely celebrate his heavenly existence.

Yet it is not uncommon, as happened following the Christchurch earthquake of 2009, after the airing to the media of such sentiments about not needing buildings, for the church to construct with indecent haste a new cathedral at the cost of millions of dollars. Moreover, the high-end design and construction teams are at work well before the parishioners – and the rest of the thousands of displaced citizens – have moved out of emergency accommodation, which can be as basic as tents and portaloos in a park.

What, then, is the relationship between a God who is purported to exist independent of buildings and the immodest rush to construct new buildings? What is more, why are church buildings deconsecrated when they pass their use-by date as if the building itself has an intimate relationship to whatever the idea of God represents?

Typically, schismatic faiths (famously the Protestants at the beginning of the Reformation) announce they will reject built structures in favour of simple congregational gatherings or even a one-on-one relationship with their God. Yet, no congregation of believers manages for long without the assistance of at least a consecrated niche or a ring of stones if not magnificent cathedrals and cloisters and ancillary buildings covering many hectares – as happened after the death of iconoclast Francis of Assisi.

All this makes sense if their God is seen as being merely an intensely felt mind-based sensation that has no existence outside the human skull. No wonder, then, that those who want to believe their God is transcendental – somewhere beyond the human body in space and time – resort to buildings to sustain the illusion he is anything but a byproduct of their most cloistered cranial interstices.

Goddesses, Gods or the biblical mono-God, were once imagined to reside on Mount Olympus or in the vicinity of Mount Sinai, and then believed to inhabit the heavens beyond the clouds. However, as astronomy peered further into space, the deities shifted house to live ever more remotely beyond the outer reaches of inter-planetary orbits until the only site remaining was completely beyond inter-galactic space. However, the brilliant irony is that all the time 'He' – or 'She' – has been cowering in the confines of the human skull.

The pathetic irony resides in the realisation the monotheistic God of the Bible does not create the world, but that human beings create 'God' every time they invoke His name or refer to the book they write or gather in buildings they construct to give Him existence outside the human cranium. Without the frequent invocations such as 'God bless', 'God be with you' or (heaven help us) 'In God we Trust', God ceases to exist – except as an unworded, unbuilt, forever internalised intense sensation of the human mind.

In complete contrast, nature requires no special creation, no salutation, no contrite pleading, no commandments – and to the point of this section – no structures or images to cause it to exist or to ensure its continued existence. Hence, it is patently evident why believers in an invisible God build 'Him' purpose-made buildings in which they congregate every time they wish to worship 'Him'. Worse, they readily become violent or even genocidal if nonbelievers challenge or mock their manically elaborate fantasies.

I confess my awareness of the God/builder syndrome was piqued when separate visits from two Christian friends during a building program on our property led not to their usual proselytising conversations but to hours of discussion about the intricacies of the buildings under construction. In further conversations with either of them, I found the mere mention of building activity would again divert them immediately from their usual religious enthusiasms.

It seems the only way to encourage God out of his hiding place in the human mind has been to construct more and more magnificent edifices in the belief he would be happy to show himself at some future undisclosed eschatological time so long as the buildings have no other function than worshipping his Immanence. All this is conditional of course on nature's willingness to let the monuments survive the next earthquake or hurricane or tornado.

The idea of God depends on linear minded technocrats who require a male-based manifestation to assuage their psychological angst about being an offshoot of a female-based species. Yet, there exists a revealing acknowledgement God remains marooned in the human mind without the willingness of builders to fabricate a public façade. Moreover, the evidence does not come from anecdotal or incidental suspicions about the reason why believers build churches.

Rather the self-reflexive job descriptions of both the biblical Creator God and his blessed Son Jesus Christ reveal their true location is in psychological sensations and fantasies of the human mind. The biblical descriptions of the two male deities are explicit about their dependence on wood, hammer and nails to get an extra-cranial manifestation.

Is it a measure of the significance of built structures for the manifestations of God the Creator/Architect's presence that the New Testament assigns God's son Christ the trade of Carpenter? Is Christ, then, not only the Son of God, but also symbol of the need for construction to fabricate the otherwise invisible manifestations of God on Earth? Why is Christ labeled a Carpenter rather than a Rabbi or other religious profession, or any other trade?

God's Son Christ, when apparently visiting Earth, further compounds the building symbolism when he declares 'Thou art Peter and upon this rock will I build my church'. While many – particularly Catholics – rejoice in the pun on Peter derived from the Latin Petrus meaning rock, they seem oblivious to the comical implication that Christ the Carpenter self-identifies himself as needing to be made visible in built form on the back of his leading disciple.

Then, as if to drive home the point, Christ is crucified with the tools of his trade – wood, hammer and nails. The Christ who is killed by carpentry metaphors then disappears for three days back into the cranium he originated from only to reappear resurrected on Sunday. It is as if he says, here boys is the way to get me out of your heads and make me appear real – use the tools of my trade and martyrdom.

Without God the Creator or Architect, Christ the Carpenter and Peter the Rock, the edifice of the Christian Church as a manifestation of the divine presence would not get off the ground – or out of our heads. God, Christ and Peter as deeply symbolic mind-based constructs would be forever circling around the brain unable to make themselves known – not even to themselves.

The act of building to materialise the biblical God does not recognise a pre-existing heavenly Maker, but the idea of God the maker idealises the universal urge to construct edifices – particularly to encapsulate the ideal building in ecclesiastical structures. Idolatry in this context is the conflict or tension between the ever-absent God and the need to manifest His presence in the only way he can exist – courtesy of built structures or imagery.

Another pertinent experience I recall was entering Saint Peter's Basilica in Rome and having the overwhelming sensation I was in God's Tomb. One of the problems for a God whose only existence is as a deeply felt sensation in the human mind is that as soon as the believers in his cosmic presence build churches to commemorate His divine omnipresence he begins to die. Or, better, the attempt to bring Him to life in bricks and mortar like any reified expectation is dead even before it begins.

Hence, the rapid rate at which new generations of hopefuls replace previous religious manifestations as they atrophy – even if some religions survive comatose for a few thousand years. Iconoclastic moments in the destruction of previous emblems of eternal life support systems give way to new periods of iconographic intensity.

The logical difference between the singularity and universality of nature and a simplistic and effervescing God ensures that when monuments to belief disappear then God disappears – except from the inner recesses of the mind. If humankind becomes extinct then God goes extinct. However, in stark contrast nature remains ever-present and indestructible.

6) Non-linear and Linear

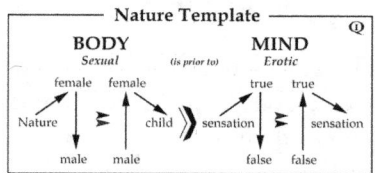 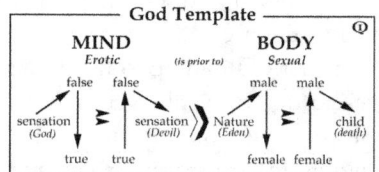

Any story, myth, or even scientific theory that posits a beginning and an end unavoidably or logically self-identifies as a linear mind-based construct. It matters little whether it be an ancient belief in an idealised Elysium beyond earthly vicissitudes, or a biblical trajectory from Creation Day to Heavenly Judgment, or a modern scientific belief in a cataclysmic Big Bang that ends in a contracting Universe.

Whatever form they take, the repurposing of such linear constructs indicates the presence of an underlying syndrome. It seems, despite the persistence and gravitas of the imagined beginnings and ends, the linear scenarios are little more than psychological ploys to allay the apprehension some experience in accommodating their perception of nature as irredeemably non-linear.

What then, does it mean to say nature (as the logical and etymologically singular given for all other possibilities) is neither non-linear nor linear – or is both linear and non-linear? How is it possible for nature to elicit both an apprehension of non-linearity and be the repository for the possibility of construing and then utilising the numerous forms of mind-based linearity?

Typical of such purpose-made linear constructs are scientific laws, mathematical equations, algorithms, fractals, digital systems, computers and even the idea of a one-way journey – or effective suicidal trip – to Mars. The common limitation of each of the linear constructs is an inability to map accurately – without adjustment or correction – onto the natural world.

More significant for societal and cultural purposes are the linear mind-based constructs that form the basis for, typically, the male-God mythology of the Bible. Moreover, there are consequences for all the spin-off biblical religions from Judaic, to Christian and Muslim – and their multitude of sectarian branchings. As such linear beliefs are endemic to human psychology-cum-philosophy, little wonder it proves difficult for many to see clearly the relationship of their mind-based and frequently male-based constructs to nature.

Shakespeare is the only thinker ever to have appreciated fully the logic of the syndrome and to have given it precise expression in the 1609 *Sonnets* and explore its ramifications in his 1623 *Folio* of plays. Moreover, the *Nature template* we derive readily from the *Sonnets* is a biological/logical explanatory tool for analysing the many linear mind-based/male based conundrums.

The rationale behind the desire for physically or metaphysically defined starting points and finishing lines can be found by consulting the *Nature template*. When mind-based constructs – and male-based religions typically – are fabricated around the trajectory from life to death for individual humans on planet Earth, aspects of the neglected first or *Body* part of the *Nature template* are incorporated involuntarily and illogically into mind-orientated beliefs and expectations.

The evolutionary non-linear birth/death cycle of human life in nature is absorbed and transformed – despite the linear mind-set overtly disparaging or rejecting it – into the linear beginning/end or life/death scenarios of metaphysical anticipation. The non-linear natural dynamic of procreation reduces to a linear simulacrum devoid of natural prerogatives as believers transform them artificially into imaginary surrogates.

What may have originally arisen as a mind-based response to natural contingencies, in the hands of those alienated from the dynamic of the *Body* portion of the *Nature template* by excessive male-based and/or mind-based inclinations, becomes an overblown substitute that cuckoo-like ejects its natural counterpart from human intellectual intercourse. Ironically, the truncated natural birth/death dynamic in mind-based myths and theories reasserts itself in the life/death myths developed to assuage the fears and hopes of mind-marooned thinkers and dreamers.

Shakespeare's nature-based philosophy as evident in his *Sonnets*, plays and poems – and crystallised in the *Nature template* – shows clearly the syndrome while providing a unique tool with which to rectify its worst manifestations and consequences.

Not only is the conceptual apparatus of linear constructs an artificial replica of the natural dynamic of procreation (or increase as Shakespeare calls it), the language of all mind-based replicas of the linear-neutral birth/death trajectory mimics their natural counterpart. In the linear imagination,

Goddesses and Gods as well as universes are born and inevitably die, and are then reborn as they experience multiple deaths as the mind engineers linear scenarios for the benefit of its eschatologically hopeful adherents.

Also visible within the *Body* portion of the *template* is the impetus that drives not only linear mind-based expectations but also linear male-based religions. The sexual differentiation of male from female in nature creates a divide between the non-linear female and the linear male.

The generic female is non-linear because she is the repository of the creative potential realised in the birth/death scenario. The capacity of the female of many species to undergo parthenogenesis – and its residual potential in the human female – points to the originary female's non-linear status.

By comparison, the female's linear male offshoot needs to return to the female to reproduce in a non-linear manner. Left alone or standing alone, the male reveals his linear susceptibility to the life/death beliefs instead of accepting the non-linear evolutionary birth/death trajectory. Hence, the inversion of natural propensities in linear constructs explains why male-based religions are always linear in their eschatological promises to believers.

Similarly, in ignorance of the natural logic of life Shakespeare uniquely structures into his 1609 *Sonnets*, science and mathematics are also subject to linear trajectories and delusions. Fundamental to – and symptomatic of – the mind-based conceits underpinning evidential science and scientific speculation is the elaborately constructed edifice of mathematics. Moreover, the two mathematical constructs that best characterise the artificiality of all such conceits are the concepts zero and infinity.

Significantly, humans invented zero and infinity only a few centuries ago to aid in the process of mathematical computation. As pure mind-based constructs, they have absolutely no counterparts in nature. Yet populist scientific theories such as the Big Bang are predicated largely on speculation about the physics of a barely known universe made artificially constant by the concepts zero and infinity. The creation of the universe from nothing in a cataclysmic Big Bang and its infinite expansion to fill ever-increasing space is entirely a construct of an manically linear imagination.

Even the claim $1 + 1 = 2$ might be true in all possible worlds, as some rationalist thinkers believe, resolves itself into the equation $1 + 1 - 2 = 0$ showing the faith in providential mathematics is a matter of belief not fact.

The similarity between the conceits of discrete beginnings and ends in science, mathematics and religion is simply a consequence of misunderstanding the relation between true/false in the *Nature template* and the consequent implications for inner sensations of the mind.

Besides the need for constants like zero and infinity to make mathematics finite and hence calculable, the inadequacy of pure mathematics to describe accurately the simultaneous singularity and complexity of nature is evident in the invention of non-linear mathematics. In contrast to simplistic mind-derived linear systems, all processes in nature are inherently nonlinear with the consequence that non-linear systems readily seem chaotic, unpredictable or counterintuitive.

The confusion affects entries in the online encyclopedia Wikipedia, where linear systems are said to hide some phenomena such as chaos and singularities. Hence, to some, aspects of the behavior of nonlinear systems appear to be counterintuitive, unpredictable or even chaotic. However, Wikipedia avers that although such chaotic behavior may resemble random behavior, it is absolutely not random.

Indeed, Wikipedia acknowledges, non-linear problems are of considerable interest to engineers, physicists and mathematicians and many other scientists. In mathematics, since nonlinear equations are difficult to solve, linear equations commonly approximate nonlinear systems. Yet this works well only up to a point.

Those who prioritise linear thinking over non-linear/linear possibilities tend to characterise the non-linear as somehow defective or troublesome as if the lack of fit that blights linear systems is the fault of non-linear eccentricities. Typical is the invention of Chaos Theory where instead of accepting that linear systems generate the sense of chaos, theorists attribute chaos to those seemingly random events and eventualities that do not fit linear models.

Yet, by consulting the *Nature template*, it is immediately evident that nature incorporates both linear and non-linear possibilities. Moreover, the set-to between the linear and non-linear is purely a consequence of inventing mind-based constructs – whether religious, scientific or mathematical – and then feeling piqued because they do not accommodate or characterise the whole of nature.

This also explains why the Wikipedia entry contradictorily considers the non-linear as chaotic and yet not random. It is chaotic viewed from the mind-based perspective of linear constructs yet is not random because there is nothing in nature outside the human mind that is ever or logically random.

The equivocation in the Wikipedia entry is symptomatic of male-based/mind based pedagogues wanting their neatly formulated constructs to be universally true. Yet as creatures who are unavoidably part of nature, they cannot but sense there is something wrong with their overwrought expectations.

7) Fact versus Fiction

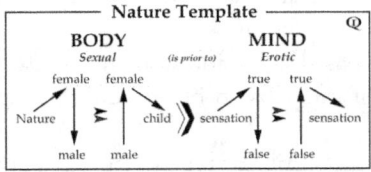 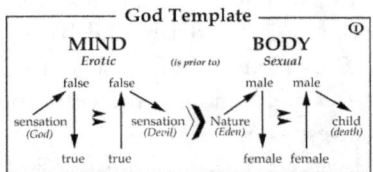

What is it about religious belief that provides its adherents with the most ecstatic mind-based epiphanies but also foments the worst excesses and horrors humankind can visit on itself – and on the planet? Biblical beliefs, particularly – whether Hebrew, Christian or Muslim and all their sects and subsects – are incredibly seductive to a susceptible mind-set yet are only too frequently associated with unimaginable cruelty and genocidal violence.

To get a measure of the peculiar attractivity that compounds saint-like purity with satanic evil it might be instructive to consider the findings from research on the obesity epidemic afflicting those cultures subject to the processed foods available in modern diets.

Trials with rats at the Scripps Institute suggest modern processed food differs from traditional fare in the inability of the body or mind to resist particular proportions of obesity-engendering ingredients.

Researchers began by feeding rats a diet of fatty foods in one trial and then sugary foods in the next. They found that neither fat nor sugar alone create sufficient levels of habituation to cause chronic obesity. It seems rats have biological mechanisms to prevent overdosing on either fat or sugar.

So, how to account for the readiness with which those hooked on high-energy foods become excessively obese and find it near impossible to break the habit? Further research at the Institute reveals rats have no way of moderating their intake of processed foods like cheesecake with a 50/50 fat/sugar combination.

The research suggests the human body, while able to signal a sufficiency of fat or sugar consumed independent of each other, has no mechanism to sound the alarm when humans indulge in the artificial combination of 50/50 fat/sugar over time. Street trials seem to confirm that foods with the 50/50 combo, which do not occur naturally but have proliferated over the last few decades, are the ones food bingers find the most difficult to resist.

Whatever the soundness of the scientific research into the effects of fat and sugar, and its applicability to the obesity epidemic, when researchers talk of wholly artificial foods that have no natural correlates, a comparison with wholly artificial mind-based beliefs is tempting.

What if, instead of fat/sugar (or body-based seductions), the relationship of fact and fiction in the constitution of mind-based beliefs and theories is investigated?

Even when the examination is cursory, a particular type of thinking and writing – all the way from religious texts to 'fantastic naturalism' novels and even conspiracy theories – seems to depend on a 50/50 mix of fact and fiction to beguile adherents and devotees. Is there an explanation in the fat/sugar 50/50 dependency of rats and humans as to why there is an equal mix of fact and fiction in both the Old and New Testaments – and other religious texts across the world's cultures?

It may seem odd that the Bible, as a witness of God's words for his chosen people, the Hebrews, intermixes mythic writings patently not based in verifiable facts and factual accounts of significant events chronicled in Hebraic history.

For instance, the Creation myth in Genesis about the formation of the world and 'mankind's' place in the world and the eschatological myth of Christ redeeming 'mankind' – are all buttressed by fantastic happenings such as virgin births, extreme longevity and miracles, etc. Yet, in and around the myths, etc., are interwoven far more credible historical accounts of kingdoms, successions, the flight from Egypt, the story of David and Goliath and others.

Yet it is the whole Bible – myth and history – that believers venerate and swear on as the whole truth and nothing but the truth, and not just the more Godly portions. Together, the patently imaginary events and the historic accounts combine to provide the basis for the Books that form the modern Bible.

Even on cursory examination, it is apparent the Bible combines fact and fiction in something like a 50/50 ratio. It is as if by interlarding fact with a similar amount of fiction the scribes knew intuitively or possibly knowingly that a susceptible and suggestive portion of the population has no resistance to the beguiling fact/fiction combination.

In its day-to-day operations, the human mind is quite capable of recognising or distinguishing facts from non-facts. Moreover, it will accommodate an intensive imbibing of facts up to the point when it is inclined to resort to fiction. It is not uncommon for a laboratory researcher, for instance, to turn to novels or movies for relaxation.

Similarly, an excess of fiction or virtual reality incites a resort to facts or just everyday activities. The continual gyration between fact and fiction in day-to-day thinking and action is both informative and productive. It provides a sound platform for organised life and an imaginative and inventive basis for discovering ways to adjust and modify circumstances to suit real and perceived needs.

Significantly, the 50/50 combination of fact and fiction in religious belief (or any virtual reality scenario) appeals to an aspect of the mind where artificial constructs have no counterpart in nature. The mind effectively has no mechanism to counter readily the seductiveness of the evenly blended fact/fiction ratios.

The consequence can be ecstatic belief unmoderated by natural prerogatives – as in monastic seclusion from procreative imperatives. Alternatively, the mind, when confronted with an artfully contrived combination of 50/50 fact and fiction, having no mechanism to ameliorate rationally the unmoderated beliefs, is readily seduced into unconscionable hate and violence.

While books like the Bible exhibit the deepest and potentially most pernicious examples of the 50/50 fact/fiction scenario, there are many lesser instances of the deceptive combination in literature and thought. The above-mentioned 'fantastic naturalism' uses the syndrome to entertain minds with stories that combine equal parts fantasy and reality.

Authors such as A. R. Tolkien, J. K. Rowling, Elizabeth Knox, Juan Luis Borges and many film directors like Stanley Kubrick, George Lucas and Peter Jackson seem to know intuitively or intentionally they can gross billions of dollars by providing such material to a susceptible and gullible audience.

Apparently sane thinkers also fall prey to the 50/50 combo in the plethora of conspiracy theories that spring up around events or writings in which there is an element of uncertainty or mystery. The conspiracy theorists fill in the missing facts with fantastic postulates creating a gerrymandered answer for those who are unwilling or unable to get a sufficient perspective on the issues or are at odds with the intellectual and artistic depth of the writings.

Major disasters, high-level assassinations, space phenomena, etc., draw those with the requisite mind-set into both endless speculation and doggedly held beliefs despite the available evidence overruling their speculations. Doubts incited by interlarding quantities of fiction to throw doubt on known facts readily dissemble natural cautions. The tenacity with which conspiracy theorists hold to their patently inadequate scenarios is explicable if their susceptibility to the 50/50 fact/fiction syndrome is acknowledged.

The connection between the biblical 50/50 fact/fiction gullibility and the willingness of those holding to such beliefs to be beguiled by politicians and others preaching half-truths or alternative facts becomes patently obvious. When politicians, for instance, continually interlard their claims with dubious facts, there is a constituency of believers already predisposed to be swayed by such devious propaganda.

The writer most subject to conspiracy theories is William Shakespeare. In all instances, the inability of the perpetrators to understand his works drives the syndrome. To compensate for feeling bewildered by their ignorance of his nature-based philosophy, so-called scholars take his extant works and interlard them with fictions about emendations, authorship theories, or reattribute parts of his works to other authors on technologic samplings.

The immense irony is that the very philosophy they are unable to appreciate provides the most effect tool for revealing the inadequacy and rationale behind their behaviour. Those who claim to love his works treat no other thinker anywhere as cavalierly as they do Shakespeare. They have the temerity to alter the sonnets and plays to conform with their own inadequate paradigms or belief systems – in Shakespeare's case most often the Christian faith.

If the effect of the 50/50 ratios remains unknown for either body or mind, then the human being lacks a powerful tool for assessing the nature of the problem and formulating responses to prevent or overcome the deleterious effects of both bodily and mental obesity.

Both the fat/sugar and fact/fiction scenarios can be illustrated and analysed using the *Nature template*. The relationship between highly processed foods and similarly manufactured religions and theories suggests the problem lies in an ignorance of the natural components of the *Nature template* and their logical or evolutionary relationships.

8) Sex versus Gender

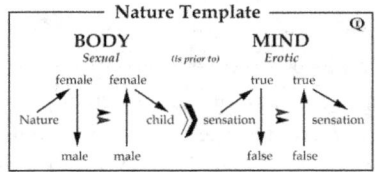 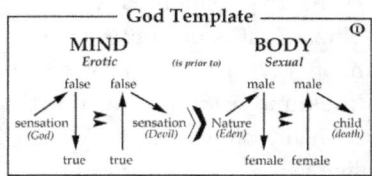

Shakespeare structures his set of 154 sonnets so that the whole set represents nature. Furthermore, he seems to appreciate that the etymological derivation of the word nature from the Latin 'natura' meaning 'birth' or 'origins' gives a linguistic and philosophical purpose to his division of the set into two sexual sequences – to the originary female and offshoot male – with the first fourteen sonnets providing the increase argument.

With the first or *Body* half of the *Nature template* set logically in place, Shakespeare then develops it isomorphically into the second or *Mind* half. Hence, the logical structuring of the mind accommodates incoming 'sensations', ideas ('true' and 'false') and interior 'sensations'. The natural logic of the body gives rise to the logic of the mind's faculties and reciprocally the mind dynamic is biologically dependent on the body dynamic.

This Section addresses the double consequence that the sexual dynamic of the body not only infuses the mind dynamic with a pervasive eroticism (as explored in Section 3) but that the female/male dynamic also gives rise to the feminine and masculine dispositions of the mind.

A direct result of the sexual dynamic of originary female and offshoot male characterising the body half of the *Nature template* is the concomitant feminine/masculine gender dynamic that characterises the *Mind* half. Shakespeare is very clear about the distinction and structures the double relationship of eroticism and personae into the 1609 *Sonnets*.

Considering the 154-sonnet set as a whole, 154 sonnets represent nature, 126 sonnets represent the male youth and 28 sonnets represent the mature female. With the first 14 sonnets presenting the logic of increase, it is apparent that the primary structuring orientates around the sexual dynamic – within nature.

Shakespeare's presentation of sexual differentiation of the two sequences and the increase argument is quite perfunctory and literal regarding the biological/logical status of sex. Only after sonnet 14 does he begin to employ erotic metaphor, pun and innuendo – with the final two sonnets 153 and 154 being intensely erotic.

Similarly, it is not until further within the set – sonnets 20 to 126 and sonnets 127 to 152 – that the feminine and masculine gender dispositions of the mind begin to play a part in creating a believable representation of their many ramifications. Sonnets 20/21 introduce the feminine-to-masculine gender characteristics of the male youth as the Master Mistress and, from sonnet 22, the Poet makes frequent reference to the youth as both an independent person and as a representative of his youthful persona.

How and to what extent, then, within the configuration of the *Nature template* derived from the *Sonnets*, does Shakespeare accommodate the range of feminine and masculine gender dispositions of the mind? Can we begin to appreciate what it is about his works that, despite their resolute nature-based logic, they attract the interest and even lifelong admiration from all sexual and gender orientations?

For instance, over the last 400 years, Shakespeare's *Sonnets* have appealed to homosexuals as much as to heterosexuals. Because of his exceptional sexual and gender inclusivity, some commentators are led to wonder whether Shakespeare himself was hetero, homo or bi – or a bit of each.

Yet it is not Shakespeare's own sexuality or gender preferences that drive his inclusivity but his consistent and comprehensive determination to base his understanding in nature – the biological source of all sexual and gender types. The ever-renewing natural biology of sexual differentiation and the consequent sex determination in the early stages of embryo development is the source of the multiplicity of sexual and gender variations.

What is the relationship, then, between the more overt residual feminine-to-masculine bodily characteristics (including rarer evolutionary types such as hermaphrodites who have both female and male organs) and the myriad of mind-based gender dispositions or preferences from heterosexual to homosexual and lesbian along with androgynous, bisexual, transgender and asexual?

Critical is the process of defeminisation toward varying degrees of masculinisation that occurs in the womb in the month or two after conception. In every developing embryo, whether with XX (female) or XY (male) chromosomes, rudimentary Mullerian (female orientated) and Wolffian (male orientated) ducts form and it is their expression that determines whether the embryo becomes male or remains female.

The XX or XY embryos require specialised genes (SYR, etc.) and hormones (testosterone, etc.) that act to suppress the Mullerian ducts and promote the Wolffian ducts otherwise the embryo exhibits originary female anatomy and behaviour – even if it is XY. While the activity of other genes (Foxl2, etc.) appear to stabilise the female embryo and its post-natal developments through to menopause to curtail the tendency to exhibit male characteristics, the male never replaces the female as the primary basis for fecundity and reproductivity.

In other words, although both defeminisation along with masculinisation and the stabilization of the female embryo must occur for a human embryo to become a viable reproductive and functioning female or male in all sexual species, the male remains completely dependent on the female for reproduction.

Shakespeare structures logically and numerologically the natural female/male dependence into his *Sonnets* 400 years ago where, without equivocation, he acknowledges the male is but an offshoot of the female. Centuries before modern science, Shakespeare could see from observing roles of female and male in childbearing, and the illogicalities of male-based/mind-based cultural and religious beliefs that the female is the precursor for the male.

Consistent with Shakespeare's natural logic, modern biology suggests the twin processes of defeminisation and masculinisation revert to female morphology and behavioural predispositions if the necessary processes to create the offshoot male morphology and behavioural dispositions do not occur. Hence, we can expect Shakespeare's works to account for both sexual morphological differentiation into female and male persons and gender behavioural differentiation into feminine and masculine personae.

The evidence suggests the degree to which the embryo is masculinised – or remains female if it fails to be defeminised – produces the full gamut of sexual types from outright female to fully functioning male. In between there are a range of intermediate types from partly masculinised female to partly feminised female and likewise for the male. Included is androgyny, where both female and male bodily characteristics are apparent, and more atypically, hermaphrodites, where both female and male sexual organs occur together.

As Shakespeare's increase sonnets recognise, the fully differentiated female and male individuals with their female and male gametes or reproductive cells intact are necessary for the sexual evolution of the species. All the other female/male types are a natural consequence of the degrees of transformation enacted on the originating embryo – XX or XY or other rarer possibilities such as XO and XXY – by the processes promoting the offshoot male option while maintaining female viability. While the intermediate types may not be fertile or reproductive, they add to the resourcefulness of the species in day-to-day survival and productivity – as with drone bees.

Similarly, there is a full range of feminine and masculine gender types consequent on the underlying feminisation or the secondary defeminisation and masculinisation of the human mind. Unlike female and male sexual differentiation, where at least some females and males need to procreate for the continuation of the species, the various combinations of feminine and masculine gender characteristics in any individual are not crucial for the perpetuation of the species.

Hence, there is a significant differentiation between the physicality of the sexual body and the conceptuality of the erotic mind. Consequently, in male-based/mind-based religions and in cultures where they prevail, the inversion of the body and mind components of the *Nature template* incites and exacerbates non-biological expectations. The glorification of the non-sexual or erotic feminine/masculine dynamic over the natural processes of sexual evolution reinforces the sense humans have alternative recourses to achieve immortality after death.

Hence, the imaginary biblical God, as a non-sexual or a-sexual entity, can only be symbolically female or male as 'He' is but an intimation or expression of masculine and feminine dispositions – or varying degrees of gender dispositions. Modern believers who quibble over whether God is sexually a female or male miss the point that He or She can only be differing degrees of an erotic feminine or masculine persona.

Evident from the illogicality of the *God template*, the relationships are terminally confused with the misattribution of a sexual characteristic to nominate a singular mind-based sensation as 'God'. The God of the Bible is nothing if not a misconstrued gender personification of deeply eroticised interior sensations of the human mind. The natural basis of the relationship resurfaces only if believers recover and understand the biological/logical implications of the female/male and feminine/masculine sexual/gender relationships of the *Nature template* for the body and mind.

Shakespeare's sonnets, plays and longer poems all examine and rectify the consequences of inverting the natural relationship of sexual and gender types. Either they celebrate the recovery of natural logic for the contentedness of body and mind or they detail the malconsequences of persisting with the unnatural prioritisation of gender characteristics for exhortation and exploitation.

When reading the *Sonnets*, it helps to appreciate that Shakespeare's Poet addresses a mature female or Mistress and an immature male or Master Mistress whose physical sexual characteristics are conterminously erotic feminine and masculine personae of the human mind. The mature female appears as a natural feminine/masculine persona, the male youth (or any immature female) as an overly masculinised persona with the Poet as the one who has learnt to balance both feminine and masculine personae (see sonnets 42/43, 133/134 and 143/144).

Similarly, in all Shakespeare's plays in the 1623 *Folio*, all the characters – in their immense variability of human types – on the one hand can be read as sexual persons active in their societies and cultures. However, it is equally possible to consider all the characters as constituting the multifarious gender personae or characteristics of any human mind – or all human minds.

When females cross-dress as males in plays like *The Merchant of Venice* (Portia), *Twelfth Night* (Viola), *As You Like It* (Rosalind) and *The Two Gentlemen of Verona* (Julia), they do not change their sexuality but merely their gender assignments. Their role is to implement the appropriate societal, political and cultural changes the God of the Bible proves incapable of doing. They only have to adopt the gender guise of the masculinised God and then freely doff the guise when they accomplish the gender rebalancing.

Shakespeare has his canny and cunning gender-swapping females and God-mocking males intervene because, as the sexual/gender dynamic of the *Nature template* shows, 'God' cannot act at all as he is resolutely marooned in the gender matrices of the human mind. Moreover, the unnatural contradictions and impositions of the *God template* reveal why 'He' is personally so impotent – but why his believers frequently cause completely gratuitous mayhem and murder.

9) Reverse Psychology

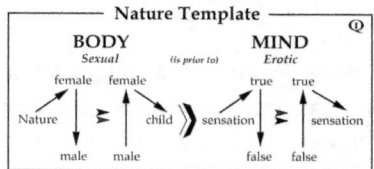 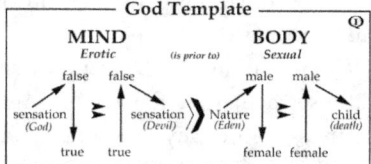

Introductory remarks

Throughout Shakespeare's 154 sonnets, thirty-six plays and four longer poems, he reveals and critiques the way the consistent and comprehensive components of the *Nature template* are converted religiously into the inversions and perversions of the *God template*. He details the implications when the trajectory from singular nature to interior sensations of the mind (the biblical deities) manifests in prejudices, injustices and violence in the patriarchal and misogynistic cultures of the previous few millennia.

In his *Folio* of fourteen Comedies, ten Histories and twelve Tragedies, particularly, Shakespeare explores the continual manic reimposition and enforcement of mind-based/male-based constructs – as typified by the *God template* – for religious and/or monarchic advantage. He shows how the mandating of such institutional measures occurs against the constant backdrop of natural prerogatives that frequently re-emerge centre stage when the overwrought constructs prove untenable or disastrous.

Consequently, Shakespeare's method is never just to recount historical incidents and precedents. After all, the accounts in the chronicles and literature most likely reflect authorial prejudices and allegiances.

Instead, all Shakespeare's sonnets, plays and longer poems make telling adaptions to the source material from the chronicles, literature or dramas. The changes he makes to the originals both correct their mind-based/male-based prejudices and reassert on our birthright nature-based philosophy.

Shakespeare's *Sonnets*, for instance, are not simply a response to or an advance on the sonnet vogue in the 1580s and 1590s. He both critiques the Romantic or Idealistic expectations of his compeers in sonnetry and develops a brilliant philosophic method based in natural logic for achieving mature understanding, emotion and expression.

At heart, Shakespeare remains true not to the chronicles or dramatised history but true to nature and our inherent natural logic, which he articulates in the 154 sonnets – as the *Nature template* makes evident.

However, Shakespeare goes further than laying down the conditions for natural contentedness and mature love. Because he understands the psychological reasons for the susceptible mind's attractivity to male-based/mind-based constructs, his lead characters act out the positive and negative implications.

In the fourteen Comedies, Shakespeare has the eleven leading females and three gender-balanced males implement strategies to forestall or turn about the deeply embedded traditional mind-based constructs. They apply natural logic to remedy or ameliorate the worst consequences for recalcitrant believers.

In contrast, in the ten Histories and twelve Tragedies, Shakespeare has the title characters – eighteen out of nineteen of whom are male (remembering seven English Kings feature in the ten Histories) – demonstrate the worst consequences of the abrogation of natural logic. He examines the fatal imposition of male-based mind-based constructs from Ancient Egypt to Tudor England to show that such cultures perennially foment rather than prevent gratuitous mayhem and murder.

To critique in the Histories and Tragedies or resolve in the Comedies an array of male-based mind-derived prejudices, Shakespeare uses incisive reverse psychological techniques. Whatever the outcome, either in epiphany or in catharsis, he directs the reverse psychological techniques towards the possibility of achieving resolution with nature-based clarity and contentedness.

Throughout the 154 sonnets, thirty-six plays and four longer poems Shakespeare uses humour, puns, comedic characters, mock arguments, mock characters, cross-dressing, fools, songs, mangled language, sarcasm, blasphemy, sexual innuendo, irony, subliminal messages and other devices. In the Comedies, the uptake by the offending characters is successful but in the Histories and Tragedies the dogged pigheadedness of fated characters proves disastrous for kith and kin.

Indicative of where the problem lies is that we talk regularly of using reverse psychology but far less readily of using reverse philosophy. For instance, a search online for reverse psychology produces many entries, whereas searches for reverse philosophy usually defaults to reverse psychology with only a refined search for 'reverse philosophy' revealing specialised usages.

Most of the usages treat philosophy as if it were psychology. The nature-based philosophy in Shakespeare's 1609 *Sonnets* is the only published 'philosophic' text that never confuses philosophy with psychology.

As the *Nature template* shows, philosophy primarily maps out the logical relationship between nature and humankind – and more particularly for the trajectory from the body to the mind – without prejudice. Philosophy, then, does not need to be challenged to reverse itself. Rather, the problem develops in the second half of the *Nature template* where those with overly idealistic expectations of mind-based constructs completely misinterpret or invert their intrinsic or natural psychology to pervert all or most aspects of the natural body-to-mind dynamic.

As argued in Section 1, the apologetic philosophy of the last few millennia is in effect psychology masquerading as philosophy. Once thinkers recognise and recover the natural logic of the body/mind dynamic then philosophy becomes philosophy without equivocation, obviating the need to make challenges to illogical thinking by using reverse psychological techniques.

Hence, the application of reverse psychology identifies psychological or mind-based consequences when the immature mind appropriates functions germane to the body as if they derive from the mind. Alternatively, the nonlinear/linear precedent of the female/male dynamic, in its impact on the operations of the mind, creates linear methodologies and expectations. These mind-based linear constructs most frequently precipitate a resort to reverse psychological techniques.

Shakespeare was acutely aware of the implications of the syndrome 400 years ago. The first half of the *Nature template* encapsulates the relationship of originary female to offshoot male. To ensure persistence into following generations the linear male has no other recourse biologically but to return to the generative female. Left to his own devices the male as the offshoot of a female-based species is an evolutionary dead end.

Because the natural logic of the originary female-to-male body dynamic transposes isomorphically onto the logic of the mind, an equivalent scenario of precursor-to-offshoot plays out. Just as with incoming sensations to the mind, what is true in language is readily verifiable in nature.

Conversely, what is false in language – or generated willfully by the machinations of the imaginative mind – requires repeated assertions of validity over time. The continual attempts to demonstrate validity of mind-based constructs – hence apologetics – contrasts with the soundness of facts evident in the world about.

Reverse psychology is particularly applicable to the syndrome where believers assert the male is the precursor for the female (as in male-based religions). It can also remedy claims by idealists that ideas generated in the mind have an independent existence apart from nature (as in Platonism).

A reverse philosophical procedure would imply the body (hence nature at large) is somehow at fault – which is patently not the case. Because the mind over body syndrome is a mind problem and not a body problem, the treatment is through reverse psychology to engineer the recovery of natural logic. The confusion is a direct result of misrepresenting our birthright body-to-mind natural philosophy.

Each of the previous eight sections examines a significant consequence in the psychological inversion of philosophical common sense. To identify the reason for the absence of philosophic clarity, we apply the nature-based logic Shakespeare articulates in the *Sonnets* for all his poems and plays.

In the plays particularly, besides the overall nature-based argument for the return to natural sanity, Shakespeare deploys characters who inject into the action moments of reverse psychological insight to point up or remedy the malconsequences of male-based/mind-based recalcitrance. His intent is to counter with an appropriate measure for measure the non-philosophic or illogical psychological excesses of traditional beliefs and speculative theories.

Shakespeare's purpose in the Comedies is to bring the plays to a successful conclusion through the deployment of canny and cunning characters. In total contrast, in the Histories and Tragedies he makes the audience aware of the failure of title characters to find a way out of their contractual quicksands or tragic quagmires.

The natural logic behind Shakespeare's micro-dramatic methods is brilliantly simple. Every reverse psychological gambit aims to unsettle the male-based/mind/based constructs and consequent prejudices and injustices ingested by his readers or audience when imbibing their traditional beliefs and misunderstandings. By jetting elements of their birthright natural logic past their ingrained misconceptions, he incites a deeply sourced nature-based response.

To correct an error or fault arising from misapplying the true/false dynamic of language that creates simplistic 'truths' (such as the fantasy belief in the existence of an extra-cranial biblical God), Shakespeare elicits a natural response in keeping with the *Nature template* and its originary female/male dynamic.

Every move Shakespeare makes is in line with the nature-based philosophy of the *Sonnets*. The humour, wittiness and/or dramatic irony evident in each play are consequences of applying the appropriate technique to remedy a particular ill or misconception.

In the Master Mistress sequence, Shakespeare discusses the idea of using small doses of a contrary belief or theory to incite a reaction that results in accepting an understanding more in tune with natural logic. In sonnets 118 and 119, particularly, Shakespeare states the principle and anticipates its beneficial consequences.

Reverse Psychology

In the plays, there are a number of instances where characters achieve their aims not by direct pleading but by stating the opposite to what the target character expects. In *Much Ado About Nothing*, for instance, Beatrice and Benedick separately overhear conversations expressing disbelief the two 'friends' cannot see that each loves the other despite their constant claims of complete disinterest. The reverse psychology Don John and others deploy is successful as at their next meeting Beatrice and Benedick accept their challenging but engaging compatibility.

In *Julius Caesar*, Mark Antony sings Cassius and Brutus' praises with reverse psychological guile. Despite their roles in overthrowing Caesar – the headstrong military conqueror who turns self-deifying despot – the crowd readily interprets his eulogy as a call to hunt Cassius and Brutus down.

Clowns

Shakespeare's appreciation of the potency of humour as a tool to dislodge traditional adolescent beliefs and attitudes is evident in his deployment of Clowns to present his nature-based philosophy. He uses humour throughout his plays, even interjecting passages of hilarity into the mordant lives of the seven kings in the ten Histories and the twelve unreflexive leads in as many Tragedies..

In *As You Like It*, the character Touchstone – whose parts in the *Folio* are labeled 'Clown' – acts as a lightning rod to ground the pretensions and fantasies of the homicidal younger Duke and idiotic melancholic Jaques. Early on Shakespeare has Touchstone identify the qualities that distinguish a 'natural philosopher' from the traditional apologists for biblical illogicalities.

Then, later Touchstone runs rings around the hapless Jaques by stating the logical conditions for avoiding gratuitous violence. He advocates using an 'if' as a last resort to defuse the absolutist manic dictates of autocrats and theocrats.

Mock Characters

While Shakespeare gives Touchstone the responsibility for articulating aspects of his nature-based philosophy, other comic characters merely mock through their unknowing stupidity the pretensions of their superiors. In *Love's Labour's Lost*, the Curate Nathaniel, the Pedant Holofernes, the Braggart Armado and Constable Dull – flaunting false piety, verbosity, braggadocio and ignorance – point up the deeper delusions and false hopes in the sexist monasticism of their Lordly betters.

Mock Arguments

If in some plays Shakespeare deploys mock characters, in others he has witty characters present mock arguments. As with all his reverse psychological techniques, the mock characters and mock arguments challenge and unsettle the prejudices and illogical beliefs held by Christians and other believers in the audience – then and now.

In *The Two Gentlemen of Verona*, Speed twice engages his fellow characters in set pieces of mock argument. First with Protheus and then with Launce, Shakespeare has Speed take a swipe at the 'Shepherd/Sheep' and the 'Jew/Christian' imagery from the Bible. Speed uses traditional syllogistics to prove nothing but that the premises of valid or apologetic argument come to nothing because they are not naturally sound.

The audience watches as two gentlemen, Valentine and Protheus, and their girlfriends, Julia and Silvia, struggle to orientate themselves to their roles in life (with only Silvia manifesting a vestige of soundness). The audience hears Speed's mockery of traditional valid argument in the context of Shakespeare's sound argument from the overarching nature-based philosophy that structures the whole play. Each of the characters is an argument place in Shakespeare's larger purpose that leads, at least in the Comedies, to a natural resolution.

In *Twelfth Night, or, What You Will*, where Shakespeare criticises the epiphanous belief in a transcendental Christ-child, he has Feste the Clown mention the word 'Syllogism' as he mocks traditional argumentative processes. Feste runs syllogistic rings around moribund Olivia as she struggles to justify her religiously morbid and morose mourning of her brother and father.

Later, Feste tells the romantically marooned Duke Orsino he would rather be told he is an 'Ass' by his enemies than be praised by his friends. As Orsino absorbs the apparent contradiction, the resulting enlightenment frees him from his lovesick doting on Olivia and prepares him for a mature relationship with Viola.

Fools

Shakespeare also deploys fools who knowingly reflect back the megalomania and malconsequences of headstrong dictators. In *King Lear*, the Fool, who acts as a foil to the egotistical and murderous Lear, is able to mirror his grossness and unfairness, but is unable to avert the utter tragedy consequent on Lear's male-based mind-based tirades and impositions. The Fool, as a persona of Lear who dies in synchronization with Lear at the end of the *Tragedy of King Lear*, lacks the natural logic enjoyed and employed by Touchstone and Feste in their Comedies.

Mangled Words

Shakespeare also employs characters such as Pastor Evans in *The Merry Wives of Windsor* and Captain Mackmorrice in *Henry V*, with their Welch and Irish accents, to mangle words central to the beliefs of his audience. Both characters highlight the critique Shakespeare makes of biblical beliefs that drive the lunacy of Falstaff in his pursuit of the two wives and the warmongering of Henry V.

In the first Scene in his play, Evans interjects the word 'Got' a number of times – and one 'Christians' – to unsettle the language expectations of Shakespeare's largely English audience. While the whole play addresses the Christian patriarchy and sexism that allows Falstaff to impose his grossly unwanted sexual advances on Mrs. Ford and Page, Shakespeare continually reminds his audience of his intentions through the verbiage and antics of minor characters.

Similarly, in *Henry V*, Mackmorrice interjects the word 'Chrish' – and one 'Christ' – a number of times in conversation with the English Captain Gower, the Scottish Captain Jamy and the Welsh Captain Fluellen. In a play in which Michael Williams will soon challenge Henry V's right to wage gratuitous Christian war for personal monarchic advantage,

Shakespeare has minor characters mangle the jingoistic Christianised language of Henry's England.

Cross-dressing

Whereas the reverse psychology of mangled language by minor characters adds to the background effects of the many tactics Shakespeare uses, when some of his leading female characters in the Comedies cross-dress to effect a complete turn-about of biblical prejudices and injustices their reverse psychologising is forefront and central to the meaning of their plays.

In *Twelfth Night, or, What You Will* Viola cross-dresses as Cesario a male eunuch to effect a sea-change in the melancholic Illyrian culture from the transcendental expectations of Christ's Epiphany (*Twelfth Night*) to the democracy of mature choices (*What You Will*).

In *The Merchant of Venice*, Portia cross-dresses as Balthasar, a lawyer, to show that God's mercy is an impotent chimera and that a dose of natural logic around the meaning of the words 'pound' and 'flesh' immediately forestalls the pigheaded a feud between Christian and Jew.

Immature and Mature Love

Another form of reverse psychology Shakespeare directs at his audience is the contrast between mature love and immature love. In *The Merchant of Venice*, Jessica and Lorenzo provide the perennial immature form of romantic love in contrast to the mature nature-based love Portia brings to her relationship with Bassanio – although he goes through a steep learning curve as he struggles to match her emotional depth.

In *Much Ado About Nothing*, the more idealistic and then jealous relationship between Claudio and Hero is the foil for the maturity of love awaiting the more feisty and circumspect regard evident in the love-match between Beatrice and Benedick.

In *Twelfth Night*, Olivia and Sebastian are the lachrymose Christian pairing married off before the play's end. Their psychological love lacks the depth and range of the mature love through natural logic Viola is able to instill in the previously romantically blinded Orsino.

Subliminal Messages

Shakespeare involves Portia in another reverse psychological strategy in *The Merchant of Venice* when she laces a song with subliminal messages to ensure Bassanio chooses the correct casket. As a victim of her recently dead patriarchal father's misogynistic will, Shakespeare has Portia demonstrate a way out of her predicament. Throughout all his plays he typically inserts subliminal messages to cue the audience to his intended meaning.

Pithy Songs

In other plays, Shakespeare uses songs to amplify messages inherent in the meaning of the play. The song that ends *Twelfth Night* appears to mock the baby Christ of the Epiphany in its first couple of stanzas and then leads to audience through to a meaning in sympathy with the play's natural logic.

To a different end, in *The Merry Wives of Windsor*, Shakespeare has Pastor Hugh Evans interlace his meandering locutions with excerpts from Christopher Marlowe's *The Passionate Shepherd to His Love*. Shakespeare intensifies his mordant nod to Marlowe's stargazing sensibility by having the words of the song recited by a verbose Christianiser.

Furthermore, Shakespeare's reverse psychological mock of Marlowe as an inferior poet, from the mouth of the garrulous egotist God-fearing Evans, predates by 400 years the stylometric idiocy of the latest edition of the Oxford *Shakespeare Complete Works* where the editors assign parts of the three *Henry VI* plays to Marlowe.

Sexual Innuendo

Throughout his plays and poems, Shakespeare uses sexual innuendo to jet ideas past the censorship of his prurient auditors in the Globe or elsewhere. In *Hamlet*, Hamlet begins his alienation from his bedmate Ophelia by heightening the erotic dissociation. He uses phrases like 'country matters' and words like 'nothing' to refer wittily to her genitalia.

In *All's Well That Ends Well*, Shakespeare intensifies the interplay between Parolles and Helen in an early exchange when Parolles uses sexual innuendo to counter her sainted expectations. Parolles gives her a racy reminder of the logical rootedness of 'rational increase' in the lives of every human born and every human who will be born in the future – including her offspring with Bertram. The innuendoish lesson in the basics of life is in keeping with Helen's use of a bed trick to dupe Bertram later in the play and overcome his heady resistance to her ungentrified origins.

Dramatic Irony

As a reverse psychological gambit, Shakespearean irony pervades all his works. He twists the conventional beliefs of his audience so the staid outcomes expected in traditional dramas are turned around completely.

In *The Winter's Tale*, Shakespeare intensifies the dramatic irony when Polixenes who, even under intense provocation from Leontes, acts rationally in the first half of the play, but proves equally capable of patriarchal murderous rage in the second half. The deep irony is that their psychological unpredictability derives from an overly-idealistic innocent childhood together.

Once they inherit the Kingdoms of Sicily and Bohemia, respectively, their immaturity of judgment resurfaces when Leontes first threatens the life of his wife Hermione and baby daughter. Then sixteen years later Polixenes threatens to murder the same daughter who is now in love with his son Florizel. Adding to the intensifying irony, Shakespeare mocks religious expectations throughout the play by secluding Hermione in a nunnery to reappear sixteen years later as a mock religious statue that appears to comes to life.

Virtual Playwrights

Shakespeare employs another reverse psychological tactic writ large when he gives a few of the lead characters in the Comedies roles as virtual directors of his play scripts. Shakespeare creates parts for them where they take responsibility for staging a successful outcome. The reverse psychology doubly kicks in when commentators, editors or directors – who reject Shakespeare's inversion of traditional biblical beliefs – take exception to characters given the responsibility to ensure a natural resolution in a dysfunctional culture.

In *Measure for Measure*, Vincentio announces early on that he will stage-manage the Christian dysfunction in Vienna, with its double dissoluteness of rampant monasteries and whorehouses. He does so, though – unbeknown to the citizens – from behind the hood of a mock monk. The irony is intense when commentators like Harold Bloom cannot temper their outrage as they pour vitriol on Vincentio – despite him having Shakespeare's complete confidence to run his play.

In Prospero's play, *The Tempest*, Shakespeare allows the reformed and repentant patriarch to establish and control a 'magical' island – an island existing only in the minds of his audience. Prospero employs the unChristian props of a zesty sprite and the misanthropic son of a witch and ends with a wedding conducted by Greek goddesses.

Throughout, Prospero implements the natural logic he learns from his 'books' and reflections after he realises his rejection of his daughter, Miranda, at birth is an indictment of his imbibed patriarchal prejudices. Even more reverse psychological is the final scene where Prospero tosses aside his 'magical' gear and sends the motley crew of Kings and Dukes back to mainland Italy to resume life as before – albeit more enlightened.

Ted Hughes, for one, could not believe Shakespeare intended to dissolve the wondrous island as Hughes imagines the blissful finale would continue hereafter. He fails to appreciate Prospero's awakening to natural logic and the role of the family group conference on the conceptual island is to establish precedents for managing future male-based/mind-based crimes in realpolitik Italy.

Blasphemy

Similarly irreverent to the traditional Christian or biblical ear are the blasphemous, and other irreligious comments Shakespeare has his cast of multifarious characters make periodically. Words and phrases like incardinate, maculate, Incony Jew, and the use of the God/dog inversion – as by Cardinal Wolsey in *Henry VIII* – cut past the imbibed sacrosanctity of Shakespeare's audience to alert their natural sensibilities.

Inferior Verse

Even poetry does not escape Shakespeare's manipulation as characters like Orlando in *As You Like It* write and recite inferior verse. The reverse psychological effect is to alert the audience, if only involuntarily, to the overarching presence in the play of Shakespeare's peerless poetic and dramatic achievement – and trenchant philosophy.

The most hilarious and revealing example of Shakespeare using versification to point up the inadequacies of biblically inspired rhyme is in *Love's Labour's Lost*. When Ferdinand, Dumaine, Longaville and Berowne fall unexpectedly in love, they all write inferior sonnets and poems to their forbidden loves.

Only Berowne's sonnet has thematic similarities to Shakespeare's own sonnets but it still lacks the deep understanding and reflexivity of the full

Nature template. Hence, the savvy Ladies consign all the Lords to a year of privation to think over their unearthly expectations and rhyming.

Sarcasm

Shakespeare even resorts to intentional sarcasm to highlight the knowing evil in characters like *Richard III* when he woos the Queen whose husband he kills shortly before. Then there is Iago in *Othello*, whose soliloquys on Othello and Desdemona reveal a level of intentionality not even the greatest of Shakespeare tragic heroes can muster. By emphasising the supreme command by such Machiavellian misanthropes of an aspect of the *Nature template*, Shakespeare shows just how bereft the other characters are of any of its elements – and why their fate is to die needlessly.

Puns

When Shakespeare articulates his nature-based philosophy, with its ensuing female/male priority and logic of increase, he uses language fully aware of its inherent eroticism devolving from its basis in the sexual dynamic in nature. Many words and phrases throughout his plays, poems and sonnets pun intentionally on the interconnection between bodily dispositions and language.

In *The Winter's Tale*, as Leontes indulges his adolescent rage against Hermione and Polixenes, Shakespeare has him pun unintentionally in phrases such as 'my wife is slippery' and 'Holy Horse' and in his frequent use of the word 'nothing'. Leontes uses language simultaneously as a weapon against an innocent wife and his friend that reveals his immature appreciation of the natural logic of language by accidentally punning on the very sexual matters troubling his adolescent mind.

Bastards

Shakespeare has parts for bastards in some of his plays – with the word bastard occurring in many of them. While bastards are central to the action in only a few plays, Shakespeare uses the compromised social status of those born out of wedlock to jar his audience through reverse psychology to reconsider their convention-bound prejudices.

In *King John*, Phillip Falconbridge, the bastard stepbrother of Robert, is introduced as the illegitimate son of Richard the Lion Heart. He is a mostly fictional character Shakespeare brings on in the first scene to highlight the inequality and injustices bastard children face – and particularly sons – in a patriarchal culture. Phillip demands his half of the properties left by their dead father to Robert. However, to avoid the unjust impositions of primogeniture he forgoes his rights in exchange for the 'honour' of being a professional soldier like his father.

Shakespeare's most exacting bastard, though, is Edmund, son of Gloucester. In the opening scene of *King Lear*, Shakespeare has Gloucester add insult by reminiscing fondly about the dalliance that leads to Edmund's bastard birth.

While Lear and Gloucester wander around the heath achieving partial reconciliation with nature – whose priorities they and their culture abuse relentlessly – Edmund achieves filial justice in the blinding of his reprobate father. Significantly, Shakespeare endows Edmund with sibling sympathy at the end from his alienated brother, Edgar.

Plays within Plays

Famously, Shakespeare has Hamlet take advantage of a visiting troupe of actors to stage a play within his play. The strategy works, both letting Hamlet prove Claudius is responsible for King Hamlet's death, and allowing Shakespeare to alert his audience to the idea *Hamlet* is but a play whose content is paramount. Shakespeare's reverse psychological intent is to expose the abrogation of natural logic that leads to murderous cultures fomented by male-based mind-based beliefs

At first, the tactic of using a play within a play seems lop-sided in *The Taming of the Shrew*, as the Induction characters of the introductory Scene do not return at the end of the play to round out the drama. However, Shakespeare demonstrates his ulterior purpose in using plays within plays when the characters in the Induction Scene make it clear their contribution merely sets the scene for the denouement of biblical illogicalities.

When Petruchio enters to tame Kate, he proceeds to rectify her male-induced truculence and restore her psychological balance by teaching her the natural logic of language. With consummate irony, Kate demonstrates at the end that she and he are free of such demeaning prerogatives.

Mockery

The most enduring example of Shakespeare's use of direct mockery to alert his audience to the gross prejudices and outright sexism in his culture occurs in his treatment of grossly simplistic Sir John Falstaff in *The Merry*

Wives of Windsor. The fact many commentators miss the nature-based aim of the mockery and continue to see Falstaff favourably as a garrulous knight-errant suggests Shakespeare's deployment of reverse psychology will always elude overly simplistic minds.

Mrs. Ford and Page (and others) shame Falstaff mercilessly three times throughout the play. First, he hides in a dirty laundry basket, then he dresses as the Witch of Brainford, and then 'fairies' mock him under an oak tree at midnight. The intensity of the mockery leads Falstaff to admit partial defeat while it provides a trenchant comment on the rabidly pejorative culture of male licentiousness and presumptuousness – then and now.

Endnote

Shakespeare's plays demonstrate the consequences of not understanding the nature-based philosophy he articulates in his *Sonnets* – and made graphic in the *Nature template*. He argues that the dramatic oversight is responsible for the largely unavoidable misunderstandings, disagreements and gratuitous violence in the politics and religions of sixteenth century society – and still occurring in the twenty-first century.

To counter the deeply embedded prejudices and injustices, Shakespeare employs many reverse psychological techniques that puncture the pretensions of believers and provide systematic methods to climb out of the adolescent mind-set of traditional faiths. Alongside the overarching argument of each play – with their nature and female-based philosophy as the basis for human understanding and expression – he provides continual provocations intended to alert or awake biblical or male-based mind-sets to their inherent natural logic and more realistic aspirations.

Concluding – How to use the Nature template

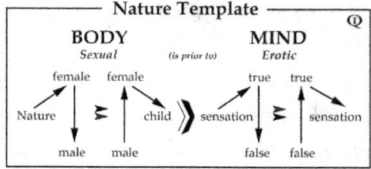 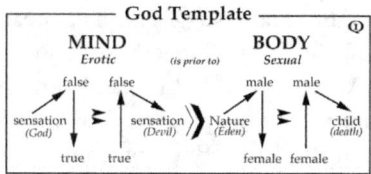

Central to an appreciation of the thinking behind Shakespeare's works – the thirty-six plays in the *Folio*, the four longer poems and crucially the 154 sonnets – is the realisation he publishes *Shake-speares Sonnets* in 1609 around twenty years after writing his first play to present the philosophy behind all his works.

Once we recognise the reality and viability of the nature-based philosophy evident in the *Sonnets*, it takes little structural or logical sense to figure out the basic components of the philosophy. The components have to be both naturally consistent and able to demonstrate the inadequacy of attempts over the last 4000 years to construct male-based mind-based systems of belief.

The *Nature template* and the illogical *God template* are both consequent on working out Shakespeare's brilliant philosophic achievement with its unmatched expression in verse and drama. The *Nature template*, as applied to many issues and situations in the world and in the human mind, proves to be unequalled as a tool for interpreting Shakespeare's works and for demonstrating the inadequacy of traditional philosophical/psychological insights and problems.

The nine topics we consider in this essay demonstrate the incisiveness of the insights inherent in the natural structuring of the *Sonnet* philosophy. They solve intractable problems besetting failed attempts to construct a consistent understanding using the inverted *God template*.

When we ask what philosophy is and how it differs from psychology, a resort to the *Nature template* immediately reveals the difference and the reasons for traditional confusions. Then we can resolve the traditional apologetic debate about the ascendency of God over nature by showing how male-based beliefs turn the *Nature template* on its head – even corrupting the etymology and meanings of the two words nature and God.

Basic to understanding the relationship of traditional culture-orientated myths to modern world demographics is the realisation all such myths are erotic as they subtend on the sexual dynamic in nature. Another consequence of male-based mind-based beliefs is their appeal to technocratic mind-sets, where the prioritising of mind-based constructs creates cul-de-sacs of technologic fantasies.

Then, by examining the name and occupation of Christ, as God-made-man, it is apparent he is a technocratic construction and tells us so by his carpentry tools and reliance on built form. Arising from the same set of expectations, when thinkers prioritise mind-based constructs, they inevitably 'create' a linear world that lacks the variety and sustainability of non-linear/linear nature.

The susceptibility of the human mind to believe fantastic scenarios as true is not a product of the illimitable human imagination but a weighted combination of 50/50 fact and fiction to which some minds have little resistance. On a different tack, only by consulting the *Nature template* is it obvious that the sexual dynamic of the body gives rise to the democracy of gender types in nature – hence why male-based religions acknowledge only male and female and confuse sex and gender.

We then itemise the reverse psychological strategies, tactics and methods Shakespeare uses to unsettle the tendency of susceptible minds to believe unreservedly in mind-based constructs and elevate them over nature. As the human genotype continues generation after generation to give birth to the same complexity of sexual and gender types, the tools Shakespeare provides from the *Nature template* to reverse psychological techniques are always viable and rewarding.

Shakespeare's 154 sonnets, thirty-six plays and four longer poems remain fascinating and beneficial to twenty-first century audiences because he appreciates that life is perennial and its excitements and developments are never ending. His nature-based philosophy remains unchanged because more than any other philosophy it accommodates all possibilities within its natural logic.

Roger Peters January 2017

From Male to Female Where the Default Lies

How the originary female is biologically constitutional, and why female priority should be politically constitutional

Two earlier revolutions in thinking

Over the last 500 years, two revolutions in thinking have dramatically upended our understanding of the world. The common denominator in each of the transformations has been the dethroning of biblical preconceptions about the Earth we live on.

In both cases, the momentous change occurs only after the evidence in favour reaches a critical mass. Until then, ideas basic to the critical shift in thinking lie dormant in the culture for hundreds of years.

The first about-face in biblical presumptions happens when Galileo turns the newly invented telescope to the heavens in the early 1600s. He confirms Copernicus' theoretical calculations from the early sixteenth century that show the solar system is heliocentric, not geocentric.

Suddenly, planet Earth, the seven-day creation of an omnipotent mind-marooned God, is no longer the centre of the world – much less the universe. Galileo's scientific confirmation of long-held speculations is so disruptive to the received view the Catholic Church places him under house arrest and forbids him to publish for the rest of his life.

Despite compliant astronomers like Galileo's contemporary Tycho Brahe manipulating the results of their observations to placate an autocratic Church, eventually the heliocentricity of the solar system – and a new understanding of the universe – predominates over traditional dogma.

The second fundamental back down for biblical beliefs comes when Darwin publishes *The Origin of Species* and *The Descent of Man*. He shows definitively 'man' is not a special creation of an almighty imaginary God – in His own image – but a species that evolves over millions of years in a line of descent that includes fishes and apes. Darwin's meticulous research, after years of observations on the Beagle and even more time studying domesticated species, rewrites biblical claims a male God creates the world – and 'man'.

Darwin's findings provide the critical mass that confirms thoughts held by thinkers since the Greeks up to and including his grandfather Erasmus Darwin. The initial response to Darwin's revelations is both acclaim at his standard of proof and dismay and denial by the Churches, some of whom hold out until late in the twentieth century before giving in to the obvious.

Again, humankind's sense of place in the universe and its fate on Earth turns on its head. Biblical beliefs held so tenaciously for 4000 years prove to be nothing than the fabrications of an over-zealous clergy and their scribes – acting on behalf of an all too human sensation called God – to assert control over a tithed congregation.

The double blow by Galileo and Darwin to male-based biblical presumptions speaks to the dogged hold on the imagination of fantastic beliefs. Moreover, the eventual consigning of such prejudices and injustices to the biblical wilderness is a reminder the democracy of enlightenment inevitably outshines blind faith.

A third about face for biblical verities

The title of this essay, *From Male to Female*, signals another defining moment in the trend to upend traditional male-based mind-based constructs. Although Galileo's discoveries and Darwin's investigations involve reversals of long held views about the universe and the planet, they do not go to the heart of the inconsistencies to challenge directly the usurpation of female priority by male impropriety.

Again, the impetus for the impending turnabout of the long-standing male/female inversion builds in the culture for hundreds of years, if not millennia. More recently, the social movement toward democratic rights for women adds its voice by challenging the great harm humankind visits on females – and males – in the name of contrary male-based beliefs.

However, it may prove that the crucial momentum for the third revolution derives not from a female but from the consistent and comprehensive nature-based female-prioritising philosophy in the works of William Shakespeare. Shakespeare, though, does benefit indirectly from female input because it seems his wife, the older Anne Hathaway, guides the younger man out of his adolescent idealism toward becoming a mature and peerless dramatist and poet.

Shakespeare argues throughout all his works for the recovery of nature-based female priority over male-based imposition of dominance. Shakespeare's previously unrecognized philosophy – hidden from view for 400 years by egotistic male-based prerogatives – provides the necessary amplitude for a third revolution. Ideas circulating for hundreds of years now have an indubitable voice that rings with irrefutable soundness.

To understand why Shakespeare's philosophy remains unseen for 400 years requires the resort to an appropriately consistent and comprehensive appreciation of how the human mind works in nature. Whereas Galileo points his telescope to the heavens and Darwin voyages around life on Earth, Shakespeare looks directly into the intellectual and imaginative functions of the human mind.

By examining the way we understand the world through the senses, language and inner sensations of the mind, Shakespeare shows why its logical functions are a direct consequence of the female being the precursor for the offshoot male in nature. Only by acknowledging the natural female priority over the dependent male is it possible to appreciate logically the isomorphic relationship of the human body and mind.

The body/mind interface is crucial for grasping the philosophic connectedness of human thinking to nature. Shakespeare's natural logic and sound arguments are incontrovertible for the relation of body to mind.

At the end of the sixteenth and the beginning of the seventeenth centuries, Shakespeare argues without demur for the originary female to gain her rightful place in relation to the offshoot male. While modern biology now provides definitive evidence the female is the precursor for the male, the scientific findings merely confirm Shakespeare's philosophical formulation of our natural female/male partnership.

In Shakespeare's day, his shift from male-based to female-based understanding and related expectations was a response to the murderous cultural debacle of the Reformation. It is even timelier now when a global demographic ensures the traditional male-dominant syndrome that induces gratuitous violence can no longer find a place to hide within the digital transparency of twenty-first century communications.

Shakespeare analyses the logic of myth

Understanding Shakespeare's nature-based philosophy requires an uncompromised insight into the deepest workings of the human mind. His natural logic relates the way we receive incoming sensations to our use of language consequent on those sensations. More significantly, he shows us how to access the inner recesses of the mythic imagination, the confusion and abuse of which generates male-based prejudices toward nature.

Galileo and Darwin's astronomical and biological challenges to the male-based mythic beliefs of the Bible do not begin to consider the logical implications of our imaginative reconstructions of the world to suit our ambitions and prejudices. Neither thinker investigates systematically the male-based mythic constructs militating against them. Instead, each remains dedicated to their scientific discoveries in astronomy and biology.

Despite the inhumane treatment Galileo receives from Pope and Church, he remains a devout Catholic – even visiting miraculous shrines for guidance. For Darwin's part, although he forgoes his Christian faith, he ruefully admits his exhaustive biological researches leave no time to muse philosophically on the deeper reasons for biblical inconsistencies.

Shakespeare, 400 years ago, uniquely examines the philosophic depth and breadth of the sensory and linguistic faculties of the mind. His advantage is that by understanding the logic of the mythic imagination – of which he is the unsurpassed master – he is able to align the natural trajectory from sexual body to the sensory, thinking and erotically creative mind with unmatched consistency and inspiration.

Shakespeare's ability to penetrate to the erotic heart of myth derives from his nature-based philosophy that contextualises all conceptual constructs. Unlike the traditional biblical myth of creation, whose geocentric orbit is sustained artificially by male-based constructs, Shakespeare establishes a global panorama based in nature for his overview of the female/male dynamic of the body that generates the natural logic of the human mind.

In 1609 Shakespeare publishes the 154-sonnet set titled *Shake-speares Sonnets* to present the nature-based philosophy behind all thirty-six plays in the 1623 *Folio* and his four longer poems. The logical structure of the 154 sonnets can be represented in the *Nature template* derived from Shakespeare's arrangement of the set.

Shakespeare bases his *Sonnet* philosophy on the external nature-to-

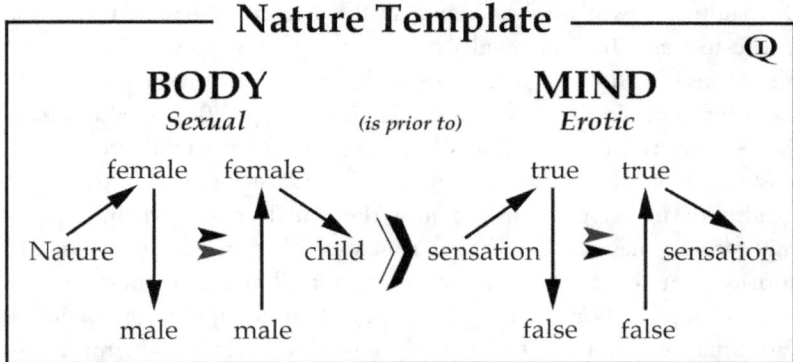

female/male dynamic that contextualises the inner workings of the human intellect and emotions. The consistent application of his nature-based *Sonnet* philosophy throughout the 1623 *Folio* of thirty-six plays and his four longer poems demonstrates the fecundity and cogency of reclaiming humankind's birthright orientation within nature.

In his day, Shakespeare issues a logical and dramatic challenge to the combative culture of Reformation sects. His plays, particularly, argue forcefully for the forswearing of male-based mind-based conflict and the recovery of the natural conciliatory partnership of originary female and offshoot male.

Shakespeare's unique combination of natural givens and thought-provoking intelligence and passion invokes from his contemporaries and seventeenth century admirers a deep but barely understood regard and respect. Unfortunately, the consequent response of blind idolisation coupled with textual interference in the *Sonnets* and *Folio* remains the Tertiary standard right into the twenty-first century.

(See earlier volumes and essays for a comprehensive discussion of Shakespeare's *Sonnet* philosophy as the basis for all his plays and poems and its implications for a global constituency.)

Marcel Duchamp independently reiterates Shakespeare's female/male mythic logic

The only other artist besides Shakespeare to plumb the depths of the natural logic of mythic expression and demonstrate his competency in a dedicated artwork is Marcel Duchamp. In the early twentieth century,

Duchamp creates a large work on glass that captures the same prerequisite female-to-male biology evident in Shakespeare's previously unprecedented insight into the natural logic of myth. (See earlier volumes and essays for discussion of Duchamp's *The Bride Stripped Bare by Her Bachelors, Even* – and his final work *Etant donnes* that repeats the mythic exposé).

While Duchamp only partially replicates Shakespeare's depth and breadth of philosophic insight into the female/male dynamic and its implications, they share the core realisation that the female's biological priority over the male has ramifications for all artistic expression. Their brilliant appreciation of the philosophic basis of myth supersedes the traditional corruption of mythic logic by male-based mind-based mythologies like the biblical.

The deep irony, an irony Duchamp recognises in comments about his own work, is that Shakespeare and Duchamp receive centuries/decades of hagiographic praise for their achievements while being completely misunderstood. Worse, while being stood on pedestals, the achievement of each is trivialised or denigrated by prejudicial alteration or misattribution.

The common denominator that drives the disturbing combination of adulation and denigration for both artists is their unflinching recognition of the originary status of the female and the derivative status of the male. The puzzling response to their works comes down to an unwillingness or refusal by admirers/dissemblers to recognise the influence of the ingrained misogyny pervading their 4000-year-old male-based mind-based beliefs and culture.

What does the science say

Scientific research demonstrating the biology of the priority of female to male is unequivocal. On all counts, the female has more attributes from a precursor asexual species that gradually divides and evolves over billions of years to become Homo sapiens – with its originary female and offshoot male.

Whether it is mitochondrial DNA, parthenogenesis, childbearing, residual sexual attributes, the default basis for genetic and hormonal sexual differentiation, gender assignments, or other characteristics, the female is always the encompassing entity for the subsidiary male. Like all sexual species, humans are biologically and logically undeniably female-based.

Most science texts and online journals, etc., acknowledge the biological priority of the female at some point. Yet it is also very common for such texts to put the male first in their considerations and representations of the male and female contributions to sexual reproduction. The otherwise inexplicable about-face seems driven by an unscientific acceptance and influence of the male-based biblical paradigm that still prevails in the culture.

Even in articles that accept the female/male priority – as in discussions about the fact only females can undergo parthenogenesis – there is usually a comforting comment at the end to the effect that males have nothing to worry about, at least for now. It is the male's universal evolutionary inability to self-reproduce that leads to the valorising of imaginary forms of cultural persistence typically in male-based religious beliefs like the biblical.

The degree to which the corrupt syndrome is inured in the culture is evident when Jonathan Miller, a noted Shakespearean play producer who is also a natural scientist, lends his name to a pop-up book *The Facts of Life* (1984) that puts the male penis and testicles before the female vagina and womb.

Since the practice of perverting, or at least equivocating about, the facts of female priority is so pervasive across the scientific literature, little wonder the literary world has not yet come to see that Shakespeare presents in his 1609 *Sonnets* a more logically – and effectively scientific – case for female precursorship.

Shakespeare's analysis of the inconsistencies in biblical myth and his recovery of a natural female-based mythic logic are as rigorous as any research by a Galileo or Darwin. Moreover, Shakespeare's nature-based philosophy goes to the crux of the issue as it criticises the philosophical apologetics at the heart of traditional religious fictions about 'man's' superior place in the world.

How far is not far enough

So, what is Shakespeare doing when redressing the biblical inversion of the natural female priority over male dominance that makes his work potentially more revolutionary than Galileo or Darwin? To put it another way, what have feminists and other activists for female rights and equality not been doing if their protests fail to spark the profound and abiding change in attitudes Galileo or Darwin's discoveries incite?

As earlier comments infer, the momentum for a revolutionary change to restore natural contingencies and overturn male-based injustices gathers in the culture for many years. When Galileo and Darwin alter so profoundly our preconceptions about the world we live in, they do not so much challenge directly the social, political or religious prejudices that characterise the inverted view of the world.

Rather, they somewhat accidentally sidestep the psychological apologia that passes for philosophy in the justification of biblical beliefs. By investigating nature at large, they recover our birthright natural philosophy or logic — however intentionally or unintentionally.

When Galileo confirms empirically the theoretical calculations of Copernicus by pointing the telescope to reveal the natural movements of the planets, his discoveries eventually overturn religious beliefs — despite own his fervent faith in an otherworldly God. Darwin, far more intentionally, uses a philosophic method completely consonant with observed facts to surmount biblical ideas about the origins and state of the natural world.

When we turn to feminists who argue for the natural role of women or for female priority, they tend to do so from social, political, scientific or religious standpoints rather than a penetrating philosophic analysis of the offending male/female doctrines in biblical myth.

Two such feminists or advocates for female rights are Germaine Greer and Riane Eisler. Greer is a polemicist who addresses issues largely through self-publicising bombast. She is far more opportunistic than Eisler who is more nearly philosophic in the cultural anthropological insights behind her writings.

Yet both women fail to appreciate the critique of male-based biblical impositions in the works of Shakespeare. Greer, as a published Shakespeare scholar, resorts to an interpretation based in Christian mythology when Shakespeare's devastating nature-based critique of patriarchal misogyny in *King Lear* proves too difficult for her to comprehend.

Eisler, rather than appreciating that Shakespeare's works provide the most thoroughgoing criticism of male/female injustices consequent on biblical beliefs, misses the sardonic irony in *The Taming of the Shrew* because she does not understand the relationship of language and sensations to mythic expression.

No previous thinker, female or male, over the last 400 years has been able to unravel Shakespeare's brilliant and consistent philosophy of natural female priority. Instead, the world awaits the realisation that in the works of Shakespeare the needed critical mass is available to transform a religiously divided world.

Why female priority is constitutional

Thomas Jefferson realises at the end of the eighteenth century that it requires a Constitutional edict to place natural philosophy at the head of all systems of belief – and no one else since has quite risen to the same level of perspicacity. He appreciates that only nature has the required singularity to correct the confusions arising from the psychology of believing the biblical God is anything other than an imaginary first cause.

Jefferson, though, like everybody else, has no understanding of the brilliant nature-based philosophy in the works of Shakespeare – and this despite his lifelong interest in Shakespeare. His Deism prevents him from making the necessary adjustments to give force to his bare intuition that biblical beliefs should be kept from becoming the basis of power in a State.

It seems timely, then, to bring about a Constitutional change to whatever set of edicts a country operates under, to include the natural fact of female priority over the subsidiary male. The resulting Act would encourage partnership rather than dominance by one sex or the other – as Riane Eisler appreciates when she institutes the Partnership Way.

Because the issue of female rights is so fundamental to our natural being, then the only just and effective way of ensuring its implementation and expectations is by including those rights at the head of a new Constitution or as an Amendment to an existing Constitution. Only then will the biologically constitutional female/male priority become the legislative and practical precondition for all aspects of a truly democratic constituency.

Roger Peters March 2017

Shakespeare & Democracy

Preamble

In what sense and to what extent can it be said William Shakespeare's (1564-1616) works anticipate modern liberal democracies where all adults, female and male, have the right to vote? After all, around the year 1600, the mid-point of Shakespeare's career as a playwright and poet, there is no such thing as universal democratic suffrage in England.

Rather there are varying degrees of theocratic dictatorship of Monarchy and/or Church across the whole of Europe with proscribed forms of parliamentary representation providing a voice for a select few. High-ranking males act as sounding boards for their monarchs or, as under Henry VIII (1491-1547), the Lords could challenge the monarch's right to act unilaterally on some issues.

Although, early in the Thirteenth Century, Magna Carta (1215) redresses the excesses and injustices of monarchs like King John (1167-1216) who claim to rule by divine right, during and after Shakespeare's day kings such as James I (1566-1625) and Charles I (1600-1649) still claim divine sanction, hence denying natural human rights to the many. Consequently, Parliament after the Restoration of Charles II (1630-1685) institutes further legislation in the 1689 Bill of Rights and the 1702 Act of Settlement to curb the abuses by English monarchs.

However, at the beginning of the Eighteenth Century the emphasis is again on restricting the hereditary and God-sanctioned claims of the now largely powerless monarchs and less on devolving greater powers on a truly democratically elected parliament. Worse, rather than finding natural common ground between all citizens, the Monarchy in the emerging Kingdom of Great Britain is reserved for Anglicans in a determined move to exclude entitled Catholics from succession.

Not until later in the Eighteenth Century – after the revolutions in France and America in particular – does the overthrow of hereditary monarchy lead to an opportunity for genuine representation for the common people. First, males become enfranchised and are able to vote for the parliament of their choice. Increasingly, states retaining the monarchy consign it to a largely perfunctory role.

After France kills off its monarchy and introduces universal male suffrage in 1792, it is thirty years into the Nineteenth Century before all adult males achieve the vote unconditionally in countries like Greece (1829) and later Germany (1871) – but not until 1965 in the USA. (While Thomas Jefferson is instrumental in drafting the *Declaration of Independence* and has a say in the *American Constitution*, which crucially separates Church and State, his and some of his colleagues support for slavery is not redressed unconditionally until after the riots at Selma in 1965.)

Although New Zealand introduces women's suffrage in 1893, across the rest of the world females only gradually gain the right to vote in the Twentieth Century. Australia (1902) and Finland (1906) lead the way but countries like France (1944), China (1949), Greece (1952) and Switzerland (1971) hold out until around or after mid-Century. Significantly, many territories including Vatican City State still refuse even limited female suffrage while Saudi Arabia is about to introduce limited voting rights for women in local council elections.

Is there a connection between females gaining the right to vote in the early-to-mid Twentieth Century and the burgeoning interest in Shakespeare's works since that time? Until thirty or so years ago, only a few of Shakespeare's plays are produced regularly and they are mostly the so-called 'Great' Tragedies like *Hamlet, Othello, Macbeth, Lear* and *Romeo and Juliet* and the supposedly lighter Comedies like *A Midsummer Night's Dream*.

Now it is common for directors to want to produce all Shakespeare's plays in their lifetimes, with every play being staged somewhere in the world in a calendar year. The inclusive approach now means celebrating all fourteen female-based Comedies from the 1623 *Folio*, particularly those in which females take a strident role in overturning male-based prejudice and injustices as in *Love's Labour's Lost, Twelfth Night* and *The Merchant of Venice*.

In contrast, by staging all twelve *Folio* Tragedies, Shakespeare's strident and persistent critique of the male-based excesses in twelve scenarios across history exposes the illegitimacy of bastardised or Christianised productions. In the not so 'Great' Tragedies like *Timon of Athens* and *Titus Andronicus*, title males manifestly head the syndrome of gratuitous mayhem and murder.

The transition from monarchical and ecclesiastical autocracy to one vote for every citizen regardless of gender, race or creed to elect a representative parliament is very much a recent phenomenon. Even today, out of the 190 or so countries in the United Nations only twenty-four can be considered fully democratic with more than fifty still resolutely theocratic and/or autocratic – as were most countries in Shakespeare's day.

If we include the various forms of democracy, then Freedom House reckons there are 123 electoral democracies today compared with just 40 in 1972. By that measure there has been a strong impulse for some form of democratic rule over the last forty or so years. Again, the increase coincides with – but we have not yet related to – the exponential interest in all Shakespeare's works over the previous half-century.

What, within the last two-hundred years particularly, changes in world politics to encourage a number of constituencies mainly in Europe, North and South America, Australasia and isolated instances elsewhere to overturn millennia of nondemocratic rule? Further, is there a common denominator between the democratic impulse and the deeply abiding influence of Shakespeare's works over the same period and now dramatically into the Twenty-first Century?

The 'Laws of Nature' and 'Nature's God'

Just over two hundred years ago the *Declaration of Independence* heralds the intent of the American Congress to dissolve constitutional ties with the British Crown. Significantly, in the desire to avoid the malconsequences of the Anglican Monarchy, two substantive concepts appear in the first sentence of the original printing of July 4, 1776. They are the 'Laws of Nature' and 'Nature's God'.

As Thomas Jefferson has responsibility for writing the first draft of the *Declaration*, the two phrases accord with his – and Thomas Paine's – expectation as Deists that 'God' may have created the world but then has no part in its day-to-day workings. Instead, according to the first sentence (which also forms the first paragraph) the 'Laws of Nature' determine the progress of the universe and life on Earth. Hence, God is no more than 'Nature's God'.

Although Jefferson is the principal architect of the wording of the *Declaration*, some of his colleagues alter the sense in places to accord with their more Christian sentiments. The second sentence, which mentions 'all men' being 'endowed by their Creator with certain unalienable rights', is less unequivocal in clearly placing God outside the Laws of Nature.

From Jefferson's vantage, the passage means that 'all men' are equal because the original act of creation makes no distinction between human beings of whatever creed. From the Christian standpoint, believers give preference to their faith as God's favoured people, a syndrome that still bedevils American domestic and international politics.

Consequently, biblically orientated history trumpets the second sentence with its alignment of the 'Creator' with 'Life, Liberty and the pursuit of Happiness'. In contrast, it downplays the significance of Jefferson's recognition of the priority of Nature over God for earthly and human affairs and his consignment of God beyond the universe – out of harm's way, for His own sake and ours.

For Jefferson the Deist, while Christianity has much to offer as a moral program, claims of Christ's divinity or intercessionist expectations through prayer or miracles are pure human fabrications contrary to the Laws of Nature. He held that religious belief is very much a personal affair and organized religions must be kept separate in law from the exercise of power in the State.

In his design for the University of Virginia, Jefferson gives graphic expression to his determination Church and State represent fantasy and reality respectively. Contrary to the traditional ground plan, Jefferson removes the chapel from its central location and replaces it with the university library to which he donates his own extensive collection of books and documents.

Jefferson's assortment of literature shows he has a lifelong interest in Shakespeare. He owns a number of complete works and commentaries on the plays and poems. His interest is such that, when he visits Shakespeare's birthplace Stratford upon Avon with John Adams in 1786, he chips off as a keepsake a piece of a chair said to be Shakespeare's.

However, Jefferson's Deism, despite its objections to Theism, still considers the deity a male. The continued allegiance to a masculine God prevents Jefferson from critiquing the male-based illogicality of biblical faiths. Consequently, his advocacy of the Laws of Nature is quite partial. Moreover, instead of making a deeper study of nature, Jefferson – like Leo Tolstoy after him – prepares a version of the New Testament stripped of its divinity and miracles.

Jefferson has no appreciation that according to the 'Laws of Nature' the originating female is the precursor for the offshoot male. If he had investigated the natural state of affairs, he might have realised Shakespeare 200 years previously articulates a nature-based female-priority philosophy in his *Sonnets* of 1609. Shakespeare's consistent and comprehensive philosophy accepts unconditionally the originating status of the female. Moreover, his plays explore the illogical implications of mind-based/male-based biblical constructs like God.

As a significant intermediary step, though, Jefferson is at least very clear about according 'Nature' its primacy and relegating 'God' to the sidelines when he and his colleagues write the *Declaration* and then prepare and promulgate the *Constitution* a few years later. While the *Declaration* invokes the 'Creator' and the 'Supreme Judge' (against Jefferson's wishes?), there is not a single use of the same words – or even the word 'God' – throughout the *Constitution* or its appended *Bill of Rights*.

Instead, there is a very clear acceptance by all parties for the absolute separation of Church and State in the Legislature, Executive and Judiciary. While religious freedom to practice personal beliefs is guaranteed to every citizen, no one denomination of whatever persuasion can be the religion of the State or any individual State in the Union – in complete contrast to the Anglican-beholden British State and Monarchy.

What emerges is a picture of human understanding at the origins of the longest surviving democratic constitution in the world, around mid-point between the end if the Sixteenth Century and the beginning of the Twenty-first Century, in which some of the worst consequences of biblically-inspired autocracy begin to be addressed. However, at the end of the Eighteenth Century, the status of ordinary folk, slaves and particularly women is still bemired in Sixteenth Century prejudices and injustices.

Europe goes global

When the young USA cuts free from mother England around 1800, it is already 300 years since Christopher Columbus (1451-1506) discovers the New World and Ferdinand Magellan (1480-1521) circumnavigates the globe.

Crucially for the events of 1800, in the preceding centuries Greater Europe is a battleground of competing biblical beliefs with Catholic pitted against Protestant and both against the Muslims or Infidels. Those who emigrate to the Colonies – and North America in particular – over the

200 years before the *Declaration of Independence*, seek to escape the worst predations of male-based religions aligned to the whims of kings and emperors.

By the end of the Sixteenth Century, Europe is caught between a blind commitment to the propriety of biblical faiths – Hebrew, Christian and Muslim – and an emerging Global constituency of heterogeneous religious beliefs. Further, as Jefferson demonstrates, there has always been a significant constituency who accept the default position of not needing the psychological resort of a religious myth.

The gradual acceptance of nature as the unquestionable given tracks from Thomas Aquinas (1225-1274) attempting to reconcile the priority of his God with Aristotle's natural world, to Nicolaus Copernicus (1473-1543) arguing for a heliocentric solar system. Galileo Galilei (1564-1642) then demonstrates heliocentricity by turning the newly invented telescope to the heavens, and philosophers like Baruch Spinoza (1632-1677) arguing that 'God' and 'Nature' are one and the same.

Spinoza, in mid-Seventeenth Century, epitomises the confusion around the status of 'God' versus 'Nature'. The grammar of the words God and nature is quite distinct and revealing. However, it will require the investigative methodology Ludwig Wittgenstein (1889-1951) develops in the Twentieth Century to see that the word God is a mind-based construct allowing of plurals and specificity compared to the singular logic of the word nature that unconditionally represents all possibilities.

The comic effect of wanting God and nature to coexist on equal terms leads some thinkers to misattribute and overcompensate as they theorise and pray God can act more singularly than he is want to do and the state of nature might prove less intractable. As a case in point, philosopher John Locke's (1632-1704) desire to validate the 'will of the people' shows that metaphysics is metaphysics whatever way you look at it.

Leading up to the 1702 Act of Settlement, Locke argues that primitive people living in a state of nature, free from external authority, have a duty to God. Locke claims further that when they 'leave the state of nature' they 'set up a judge...with authority to determine all the controversies and redress the injuries'. However, this authority is not absolute as the judge is 'answerable to the will and determination of the majority'.

Out of his presumptuousness that primitive people recognise Locke's idealised monotheistic God rather than a multiplicity of goddesses and gods in sympathy with their natural surroundings, Locke then imagines a sophisticated society in which a human 'judge' is responsive to the will of the people. Yet it is the biblical mind-based construct of a male God who is invoked as the ultimate judge in that society.

Locke inverts reality when he makes his God the recourse of primitive people while his own society has a secular 'judge'. He willfully ignores the short history of the monotheistic God the writers of Genesis invent only a few thousand years ago for their sophisticated cultures. His confusion is symptomatic of the desire to enact natural social justice while still believing in an omnipotent male God.

Even before Locke, though, the circumnavigation of the globe and the demonstration of the heliocentricity of the solar system both show biblical verities to be no more than fictions and that nature is the ultimate recourse for human understanding. However, it is not until Charles Darwin (1809-1882) in *The Origin of Species* proves that all humans are evolved from species lower in the animal hierarchy that the forces of nature completely overshadow biblical claims of God's existence and influence.

Darwin goes further in *The Descent of Man* when he argues on the basis of evidence that human 'mental powers' and 'moral sense' derive from the faculties and sensibilities of evolutionaryly related species. The idea the capabilities of the human mind evolve over time from sensate but incognitive species to fully cognitive humans demonstrates the human mind derives from bodily potentialities.

Into the Twentieth Century, the artist Marcel Duchamp (1887-1968) displays graphically in his major work *The Bride Stripped Bare by Her Bachelors, Even* or *Large Glass* the natural relationship of female priority to male reflectivity in art, and consequently for any form of human endeavor. By representing the logical conditions for all mythic expression in the arrangement and mechanisms of the *Large Glass*, Duchamp also rectifies 4000 or so years of male-based usurpation.

As the female is the precursor for the male in all species, or in other words humans are a female-based species, then the female/male-driven sexual dynamic creates the feminine/masculine-driven mind dynamic. While the male or masculine drive in the female or male generates many of the beneficial technocratic constructs and constructions, the imaginary male-based entities or Gods of mind-based biblical religions cannot supplant the originary female.

Biology of the female as precursor

The evidence from multiple sources supports the biological fact the female is the precursor for the male in all sexual species since single cell animals differentiated eons ago, hence making humans a female-based species. Consequently, the issue for the politics of male-based autocracy versus universal-suffrage democracy is not so much in proving it to be the case but accepting it is the case.

Whether by following the development of the fertilised egg in the womb where genes and hormones act on the originary female to change her into a male potentiality – or remain female, or simply by observing the primary role the female has in reproductive responsibilities including pregnancy and nurturing, the female emerges unequivocally as the precursor for the male.

By considering the significance of mitochondrial DNA, rudimentary sexual characteristics such as nipples in the male, the disposition of feminine and masculine gender characteristics and the role of secondary sexual characteristics in courtship, in each instance the generative role of the female and the subsidiary role of the male emerges.

The consequence of weighing the evidence for female priority should be an acceptance the formation of the male from the female potentiality is an act of partnership and not one of domination. The consequence of not accepting the evidence but of asserting the priority of male over female leads to expectations and strictures that enforce an unnatural imposition of male/masculine dominance over female/feminine accommodation.

The telling signs of society acting against the natural order are the freedoms aggregated to the males and the countermanding restraints placed on female liberty and expression. In male-based religious cultures, the measures instituted to ensure male dominance – sanctioned supposedly by a male God – range from blasphemy, to the confinement of women, to honour killings.

Hence, to a qualified or a casual observer, the twofold evidence of scientific findings and cultural oppression confirm the natural originary status of female to male. Yet, there are further consequences for human understanding and expression of the suppression of the female precursorship and the imposition of male priority.

While the females of some sexual species can self-reproduce by parthenogenesis, the males of no species have the capacity to do so. Effectively, the female of any species is the source of reproductive potential while the male needs to return to the female if he wishes to perpetuate himself biologically and ultimately culturally.

The implication is that the male is an evolutionary offshoot of the female created by the original asexual lifeforms to achieve goals other than self-reproductive ones. In effect, the male lacks the full capacity to reproduce himself because his role is to establish opportunities for the female other than those related to reproductive necessity.

The further implication, which is compromised or rendered void by male-based cultures, is that the male potentiality corresponds to the ability of the human mind through language to create ideas that are false, or constructs not known in nature, for the purposes of insight and endeavor. The female/male sexual dynamic corresponds to the true/false dynamic constitutional of language.

Moreover, in the most deeply realised art works, the male fulfils his destiny to the female by reflecting back to her the way she is and the nature of her relationship to him. This is the essence of the appeal of the *Mona Lisa* by Leonardo da Vinci (1452-1519), and is the principal content of Duchamp's *Large Glass* and other works, which encapsulate the mythic relationship of female priority to male representation without apology.

The irony of biblical male-based mythologies is that the male narcissistically thinks he is the object to be admired in a mirror he holds up to himself. Hence the infighting that inevitably occurs between male-based religions when each narcissicised God wishes to be the center of his own selfish attention instead of creatively reflecting the female back to her fecund self.

The alignment of narcissistic religious power-mongering with personal aggrandisement that characterises theocratic autocracies through the ages creates intolerable privileges and injustices that are usually overthrown only by violent revolution.

The remnants of such delusions and excesses can be seen in the ring-fenced Vatican State and Buckingham Palace. Yet, live instances are still visible recently in Northern Ireland and Yugoslavia as well as Saudi Arabia and some other Muslim States where male-based religion is used as a means of repression antagonistic to the democratic communion of humankind.

With the word nature occurring uniquely only in the singular when referring to all possibilities – there is no generic plural 'natures' – and the undeniability of female priority, it seems appropriate that modern liberal democracies look to nature and acknowledge the female/male partnership so that true democratic opportunities can flourish.

Shakespeare's nature-based philosophy

The trend toward genuine secular and liberal democracy and universal suffrage inclusive of both female and male is associated predominantly with cultures in which the male no longer usurps female priority. The recovery of the natural female/male relationship recognises ubiquitous nature over male-based/mind-based religious sectarianism effectively ring-fencing Gods within the constructs and constructions fabricated to externalize them outside the human brain.

The tendency toward democracy and universal suffrage has barely begun in Shakespeare's day, so in what way can it be said his works presage the shift from theocratic/monarchic autocracies to modern democratic states.

In the prefatory material to the 1623 *Folio*, John Heminge and Henry Condell say Shakespeare 'was a happy imitator of Nature' and a 'gentle expresser of it' and even Samuel Johnson (1709-1784) asserts Shakespeare holds a mirror up to nature. Considering many accept Shakespeare bases his works in nature rather than biblical Gods or Platonic ideals, it should occasion no surprise Shakespeare publishes his set of 154 sonnets in 1609 to present a nature-based philosophy.

Yet, ironically, the ability to first discern and then develop a full account of the way Shakespeare structures his nature-based philosophy into the sonnet set has had to wait until near the end of the Twentieth Century. Just over 100 years after women gain the vote in New Zealand, it can now be demonstrated conclusively Shakespeare intentionally embeds his nature-based philosophy in his 1609 *Sonnets* and he significantly acknowledges the female as the precursor for the offshoot male.

Shakespeare arranges his 154 sonnets so the complete set represents singular nature with the two internal sequences of 28 sonnets representing the originary female and 126 sonnets represent the offshoot male respectively. By allowing the readily discernable features of the set to represent nature, female and male, Shakespeare recognises they are unarguable givens that logically determine everything else that follows for the relationship of body and mind both in nature at large and within the set.

To accentuate the significance of his unique decision to address both female and male in a sonnet set of his day, Shakespeare adapts the numerological ordering system common amongst poets before and during his time to characterise his logical entities. The 154 sonnets representing nature numerologically reduce to a unity (154 = 1+5+4 = 10 = 1+0 = 1) that corresponds to the generic word nature being used only in the singular and never the plural – except metaphorically as human natures.

Similarly, the 28 sonnets representing the female also reduce to a unity (28 = 2+8 = 10 = 1+0 = 1) as the originary female has a direct relation to originating nature. Significantly, the 126 sonnets representing the offshoot male add to the lesser number 9 (126 = 1+2+6 = 9). At 1 less than 10, the 9 both acknowledges the differentiation of the male from the unity of the originating female in nature and the biological requirement that at least some males return to the female to perpetuate humankind (9 + 1 = 10 = 1+0 = 1).

To that end, Shakespeare opens the set with 14 increase sonnets. They present the generic argument that, if humankind wishes to persist, female and male need to reproduce otherwise there will be no more humans in 'three score years' (as sonnet 11 avows). Hence, the opening argument in the set addresses the logical consequence of the differentiation of the subsidiary male from the originary female in nature.

Once Shakespeare establishes the logical relationship between nature, the female/male sexual dynamic and the logic of increase, he then proceeds to explore the implications for the human mind in terms of incoming sensations, the true/false logic of language and the interior sensations of the mind. The natural connectivity between the body dynamic and the mind dynamic and the complete consistency of its implications reinforces the appropriateness of acknowledging female precursorship in nature for every aspect of human endeavour.

It is possible to configure the logical relationships into a *Nature template* that shows how the various components of Shakespeare's arrangement of the 154 sonnets cohere isomorphically. Their graphic representation in the *Nature template* provides a powerful tool for interpretation and exploration.

The *Nature template* shows the logical connectivity between body dynamic of nature, female and male, and the mind dynamic of exterior and internal sensations and the true/false logic of language. The *Nature template - Sonnets*, presents the relationships in the terminology of the 154-sonnet set to demonstrate how the 1609 *Sonnets* configure body/mind isomorphism.

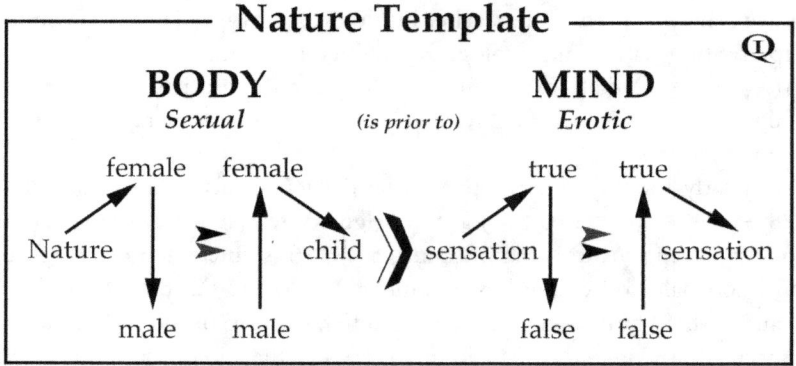

The elements of the *Sonnet* logic could be examined in detail here to demonstrate their cogency and utility. For our purposes, though, the next move is to assert Shakespeare publishes the *Sonnets* in 1609 to present the philosophy behind all his plays and longer poems. (If necessary, consult the four-volume 1760-page *William Shakespeare's Sonnet Philosophy* of 2005 or further publications such as the more concise *Shakespeare's Global Philosophy* of 2017).

The first step is to recognise Shakespeare bases the political, social and religious critique evident in the thirty-six plays of the 1623 *Folio* on the nature-based and female-precursor logic of the *Sonnets*. Then we can begin to appreciate why there is a connection between the burgeoning interest in Shakespeare's work late Twentieth Century and the growth in the proportion of countries opting for universal suffrage in liberal and secular democracies.

Shakespeare's colleagues arrange the plays in the 1623 *Folio* – most likely according to his wishes – into fourteen Comedies, ten Histories and twelve Tragedies. Shakespeare shows how to apply the *Sonnet* philosophy successfully in the Comedies to avert male-based/mind-based dysfunction while conversely in the Histories and Tragedies he examines circumstances where the absence of the consistent and comprehensive philosophy leads to mayhem and murder. The plays, then, are where it is possible to discern the relationship between Shakespeare's nature-based philosophy and some of the first inklings of the modern democratic impulse.

Not only do the thirty-six plays constantly reference nature throughout, in the fourteen generically titled Comedies eleven canny and cunning females – and three gender-balanced males – take the lead to resolve male-based crimes and injustices. Contrarily, in the twenty-two Histories and Tragedies, males named in the play titles – and a few overly masculinised females – cause political, social and religious hegemony and violence.

While there are no democratic rights or constitutional governments in Shakespeare's day, his works argue for natural justice, female rights and against the autocratic imposition of male-based politics and religions. From 400 years ago to the present day, the psychopathic excesses of monarchies, dictatorships, religions, racism, institutionalised misogyny and other impositions and exactions have been redressed gradually.

All are issues Shakespeare's nature-based philosophy provides a criticism of and implements viable remedies for both in its *Sonnet* representation and its application to a multiplicity of situations in the plays and longer poems. That Shakespeare's philosophy has remained unknown until very recently suggests the unwitting influence of his works over the period since 1600 can now be enhanced immeasurably as the global world catches up.

Getting it right about myth

Besides the recent revelation of the brilliant nature-based philosophy embedded in the 1609 *Sonnets*, another aspect of Shakespeare's achievement helps explain the enduring fascination with his works. In the *Sonnets*, Shakespeare articulates fully the logical conditions for mythic expression, hence providing a level of artistic depth and integrity in his plays and poems unknown in any other oeuvre.

The only artist ever to have similarly articulated the logical conditions for mythic expression is Marcel Duchamp in the Twentieth Century. His achievement, though, is limited by his exclusive focus on mind-based sensations or aesthetics. Shakespeare not only encapsulates the basis of all mythic writing and art, he explains how he does so for every aspect of human endeavour in the *Sonnets* and explores a range of related trenchant life and death issues in the plays to provide a truly magisterial corpus of global significance.

As a contribution to the developing momentum towards democracy worldwide, Shakespeare's works encompass the natural conditions that ensure universal suffrage accomplishes its aims. He also achieves an exceptional level of mythic depth to assuage the desires of those needing connectivity between nature and their imaginary mythological ambitions and concerns.

The realisation male-based/mind-based prerogatives when given constitutional sanction can only serve the interests of believers in a particular mythology reinforces the timeliness of the recent trend to fully representative secular democracy. The problem is not alleviated by sanctioning a grouping of mythologies such as the biblical variations and does nothing to address the dictatorial aggrandising by leaders of religious sects as typified by Catholics and Anglicans.

In contrast, by not compromising on universal suffrage, modern democracies ensure an unprejudiced resort to nature and female priority. Consequently, nature-based democracies are able to be systematically free at heart from the extreme partisan tastes and expectations male-based myths generate and exacerbate.

The United Nations Universal Declaration of Human Rights takes account of the issues. The Declaration ensures all member states unite under the banner of a mythology-free zone. Anyone can change their 'religion or belief' (Article 18) without fear of persecution, and women particularly have 'equal rights as to marriage, during marriage and at its dissolution' (Article 16).

Yet, in opposition to the freedoms the Declaration enshrines, a group of Muslim Countries insists on creating their own Cairo Declaration of Human Rights in Islam to maintain misogynistic practices and religious impositions. Worse, Shimon Peres (1923-) approaches Pope Francis (1936-) in 2014 to propose a United Nations of Religions.

Typical of those who prioritise mythological fantasies over natural prerogatives, Peres has no regard for the evidence genuine democratic representation is achievable only by taking religious myths off the political agenda or at least, as Jefferson appreciated, constitutionally ring-fencing the sociopathic tendency of male-based faiths to dominate and skew the political process.

The dramatic shift toward natural justice is evident recently in the large majority of Irish voters in a referendum who support the right to marriage for all citizens regardless of sexual proclivity. Previously, the male-based Catholic Church – in which no priest marries – dictates the sexual mores of the people. However, the contradictions and hypocrisies of a Church hiding its sexual abuses surreptitiously, while denying natural rights to homosexuals – and heterosexuals – is at last remedied by the will of the people.

When the Irish have an opportunity to express their views untraumatised by a patriarchal Church, they respond to the realisation all forms of sexuality are a natural consequence of sexual differentiation in the womb. The opportunity to listen to natural prerogatives revives the female priority and returns the Irish community to justice and fairness after millennia of religious fear and abuse.

If nation states insist on preordaining any one of the various forms of religious belief as a precondition for democracy, then the ability of the people to find effective recourse in nature and female/male partnership rather than imaginary Goddesses and Gods is severely blunted or completely eschewed.

The transition over the previous 400 years from entrenched male-based mythologies to a deeper understanding of the logic of myth for a genuine nature-based democracy is confused and confounded by attempts to forge compromises between the logically retrograde and frequently belligerent beliefs and the emerging nature-orientated female-based constituency.

Continued reluctance or outright refusal in the Twenty and Twenty-first Centuries to acknowledge biological and hence logical priorities recalls the nature/God confusion bedeviling John Locke in the Seventeenth Century. Typical is the Post-modern syndrome pervasive throughout Tertiary that dictates no language construct has priority over others.

Lost in the illogical malaise is the unique ability of the word nature to remain singular in the grammar of language for all generic uses. Whereas words like universe, world and God are mind-based constructs – each referring to a grammatically limited referent either inside or outside the mind – the word nature is ubiquitous and in its singularity encompasses all possibilities.

The grammatical blindness of the Post-modern compromise is epitomised by the assertion all colour observations are culturally determined as a consequence of being named in language. Yet, it is readily demonstrated all people see the same colour spectrum throughout nature (other than for colour blindness) despite artificial colour boundaries and grouping of colours and colours being called differing names in different cultures.

Once thinkers recognise nature as the only logically singular and universal word – and the female is the precursor for the male – then a constituency is possible that has complete freedom from the dictates of taste (with male-based myths as the ultimate in contrived taste). Only by acknowledging the evolutionary sexual partnership of female and male, and its natural correlates, can a nature-based sensibility gain a political voice.

Common ground – nature and universal suffrage

Is it a coincidence Shakespeare's works are receiving an unprecedented level of attention both in production and analysis just when democracies based on universal suffrage for females and males supplant autocracies based on male privilege and as nature-based constitutions supersede God-based monarchic and papal impositions?

Shakespeare's sonnets, plays and poems are demonstrably the only body of work to articulate a consistent and comprehensive nature-based/female-originary philosophy. This means the apparent coincidence between the recent move to universal suffrage for females and males and the exponential upsurge in staging all Shakespeare's works may be no coincidence at all.

The political shift from monarchic and theocratic dictatorships to multi-party parliaments over the last 400 years matches the contrast between the traditional doctrinaire/dogmatism of male-based apologetics and the evidence-based process of sound argument and inculcation of nature-based content and accountability.

The grounded arguments and values are evident throughout Shakespeare's works. They are structured into his 1609 *Sonnets*, and are elaborated deliberately and extensively throughout the political, social and religious scenarios he case-studies in his four longer poems and *Folio* of thirty-six plays.

The parliamentary debating chamber, where every citizen has the democratic right to have their point of view represented, now replaces the absolute righteousness of autocratic/dictatorial edicts enacted disproportionately in favour of the ruling elite. While modern democracy represents a spectrum of special interest constituencies resulting in competing party-political factions, by subjecting the various candidatures to frequent nature-based universal plebiscites the people can weigh their policies against the natural benefits and harms to both human and the environment.

The emergence of Green Parties under nature-based democratic accountability is consistent with the need for the natural conscience to have a political voice. The increased environmental awareness ameliorates the malconsequences of pure mind-based constructs driving monotheistic religions and particularly male-biased biblically sanctioned political impositions and exactions.

The current ten to twenty percent level of Green Party parliamentary representation reflects the continued imbalance between mind-based/male-based idealised aspirations that motivate economies and cultures and the need for the excesses of unfettered expectations to be subject to natural checks and balances.

With the granting of voting rights to all females and males, the ability to reason cogently now determines the voting age. Countries decide on the appropriate voting age by assessing the ability of the young person to weigh the social, political, economic and religious issues with some maturity. Currently, the majority of countries worldwide opt for 18 years while a few countries range from 21 (Fiji) to 16 (Brazil – where those under 18 and over 70 do not have to vote).

Whatever issues surface in the modern democratic system, by returning the constituency to the ballot box every few years, the recourse to nature and the originary female acts as a balancing process to rectify and remedy the tendency for one or other political faction to implement their policies unchecked by considered electoral consent. Concomitant freedoms of the press and freedom of association and the right to dissent ensures politicians can both raise objections to policy initiatives and face scrutiny if they transgress natural prerogatives.

Shakespeare, as a philosopher of unrivalled integrity and insight, predicts in his works the demise of the Monarchy, the ring-fencing of Churches, the prohibition of racism, and the universal enfranchisement of females and males. Consistent with his deeply philosophic sensibility, Shakespeare does not propose forms of political, social and religious society for the future. Rather his logical critique creates guidelines and opportunities for those faced with scenarios in the future to make decisions appropriate to their times.

Now, at the beginning of the Twenty-first Century, the implications of Shakespeare's thoroughgoing philosophic analysis and critique of social, political and religious systems at the end of the Sixteenth Century has led, in part, to universal suffrage in parliamentary democracies as the fastest growing form of governance worldwide.

Basic to any system of government arising from Shakespeare's works is the overt or tacit acceptance of nature as primary (as Jefferson appreciated around the end of the Eighteenth Century) and the originary status of the female for assessing the appropriateness and ambitiousness of policies and constraints.

Roger Peters May 2015

From Tertiary to Quaternary

CONTENTS

The Creative University   93

Criteria for Quaternary   113

Quaternary Pedagogy   125

Upgrading from Tertiary to Quaternary   133

The Creative University

Education and the Creative Economy

KNOWLEDGE FORMATION, GLOBAL CREATION AND THE IMAGINATION

The University of Waikato
August 15 & 16 2012

TOWARD A QUATERNARY LEVEL OF CREATIVE EDUCATION

Preamble

What does it mean to debate the status of the 'Creative University'? Why is this an interesting question to ask when the twenty-first century planet is wall-to-wall with centers of University education, all brimming with various forms of creativity across faculties? Is there a relationship between a University-based conference such as this and the apprehension that the University offers only specialised forms of creativity somewhat apart from the creative potential in the world? (1) (2)

The deeper question relates to the idea of a University itself, or the Tertiary level education, and its role and relevance in the modern world. We could ask was the University once considered the height of creativity and are we really in troubled times for the Creative University. If so, are there options that might allow the Creative University to be the institution that speaks more inclusively to global creativity for the twenty-first century.

In this paper, I want to outline a scenario that identifies a palpable gap between the highest level of creativity available in Tertiary and a level of creativity evident in a few seminal thinkers whose deepest work is demonstrably not yet part of the Tertiary program. My argument will be that the absence from Tertiary of their deepest insights is at the heart of the disquiet about creativity reflected in the conference title.

Discovering Shakespeare's nature-based philosophy

The thinker/artist who best exemplifies the disjunction between Tertiary creativity and the full human potential for creativity is William Shakespeare. The telling distinction lies in appreciating that Shakespeare uniquely incorporates a profound systematic nature-based philosophy in his set of 154 sonnets of 1609 to present the philosophy behind all his plays and poems.

What does it say of the philosophic basis of University education and creativity that Shakespeare's *Sonnet* philosophy has remained completely unknown in Tertiary worldwide for 400 years? The absence since the seventeenth century of Shakespeare's philosophy from the highest level of learning is undeniably the case despite the efforts of very distinguished thinkers and artists. Even those who have apprehended a profound philosophy in Shakespeare's works have had to admit their failure to discern it. (3)

The oversight is monumental for a thinker/poet/dramatist as significant as Shakespeare who still holds centre stage worldwide. Shakespeare's complete 1623 *Folio* of 36 plays is now performed often and everywhere internationally – compared to only a few tragedies and other plays performed rather pompously in corrupt versions only sixty years ago. (4) In 2009, all the plays were performed at Stratford Upon Avon. (5) More recently, performances based on his works commanded six major billings at the 2012 International Festival of Arts in Wellington. No other artist could presume on multiple exposures at one festival. (6)

I can only give a brief indication in this paper of the significance of the consistent and comprehensive nature-based philosophy Shakespeare articulates in his set of sonnets. I have produced extensive argument and evidence in *William Shakespeare's Sonnet Philosophy* of 2005 and on the Quaternary Institute website over the last twelve years that Shakespeare lays out the philosophic basis of his life-long creativity in his sonnet set of 1609. (7)

Because Shakespeare's creativity is acknowledged near universally as peerless, just what keeps Tertiary worldwide for 400 years from penetrating his lucid philosophic articulation and poetic evocation of his creative program? The answer has to lie at the very heart of the Tertiary conception of creativity.

Foundations of Tertiary

We know Universities were founded around the year 1100 in cities such as Paris and Bologna. We also know they were Christian/Catholic centers of learning that took the biblical myth of the creation of the world by a male God as an unquestionable given. One of the aims of the nascent University was to demonstrate that the biblical dogmas were not at odds with the findings of natural science, or at least were not excluded logically. (8)

Hence, around 1250 we have Aquinas arguing for God's dominion in relation to nature and later around 1650 Spinoza argues for the unity and inseparability of God and nature. (9) (10) However, Aquinas and Spinoza, and most recognised philosophers of the last 1000 years, have been unwilling or unable to both challenge and supersede the dogma of a male God creating the world from nothing. (11) As effective apologists for biblical verities, philosophers have used syllogistic methods of valid argument perfected by the Greeks to establish a case regardless of the soundness of its premises.

Many impressive buildings and works of art were created over the 1500 years from the Medieval period to the Rococo in the name of the male God. Despite the divine sanction, however, many have not proven resistant to the forces of nature. Consequently, in the twenty-first century, the Dean of Canterbury Cathedral, Christchurch, when asked about the role God had in the devastating earthquake of 2010 that destroyed the Cathedral, confessed the shaking was nature's work whereas God is evident in the love between those helping in the recovery. (12) At moments like these, the purely mind-based status of the male-God is revealed as the doctrines and dogmas that support his nature-creating reputation prove unavailing.

Critically, at the foundation of the University as an institution of rigorous learning there existed a double inconsistency of male-God priority and creation ex-nihilo – all welded together with unsound argument. Tertiary today is still afflicted with the inconsistencies. It is in a psychological bind driven by the remnants of apologetics. Effectively it continues to justify unsound precepts without a full recourse to nature as the only indubitable given.

In ordinary usage, compared to God/gods, world/worlds, universe/universes, we use 'nature' only in the singular and neither do we use it in English with articles such as 'a', 'the' or 'an'. Unlike the word God, the word nature requires no preconditions, no mandatory capital N and no special commandments to assert its status. Because Tertiary still operates under the mandate of countermanding mind-based constructs, it is unable to offer sound nature-based creativity for the increasingly nature-orientated culture of the twenty-first century.

Again, the measure of Tertiary's failure to throw off the inconsistencies in the biblical paradigm and millennia of apologetic psychology is its failure to appreciate the profound nature-based philosophy Shakespeare articulates in his 154 sonnets for a global constituency. Worse, for 300 years commentators have willfully emended, altered and reattributed large tracts of Shakespeare's works making the history of interpretation of his oeuvre one of the greatest travesties visited on the extant works of a profound writer/thinker. (13)

The upshot of the attempt to institute a University level of education based on unsound biblical precepts has been the epistemological scepticism typical of Hume or the God is Dead headline pronounced by Nietzsche. (14) Hume commented on the relationship between his sceptical mind and the absence of scepticism when performing his day-to-day activities. (15) Revealingly, for his part, Nietzsche still validated male-priority and believed Bacon was Shakespeare. (16)

The consequence for the twentieth century has been a self-referential form of creativity that is stylistically anxious about admitting it has no idea what to say. When considering the current status of the Creative University, we are all too aware of postmodernism's stranglehold on our freedom not to be postmodern. (17)

Duchamp's understanding of the logic of myth

Although, the profound problem for Tertiary creativity is at its most evident in its inability to understand the work of Shakespeare, there are three other seminal thinkers – Marcel Duchamp, Charles Darwin and Ludwig Wittgenstein – whose work has not been done justice in Tertiary. I studied these three thinkers (and all the associated literature) for 20 years before apprehending the *Sonnet* philosophy in 1995. I needed to bring together the most philosophically penetrating aspects of their specialised contributions to appreciate Shakespeare's overarching achievement. (18)

I will highlight aspects of the work of artist Duchamp, scientist Darwin and philosopher Wittgenstein that are not fully appreciated or taught in Tertiary.

To begin measuring creativity at the appropriate level, we turn to the most influential artist of the twentieth century, Marcel Duchamp. Whereas for many artists and connoisseurs Pablo Picasso and others seem very last century, Duchamp still exerts a powerful influence in the twenty-first. (19) For an artist who was the antithesis of a university Don, Duchamp provides endless fodder for dissertations about just what he was up to in his challenging art.

Typical is a recent PhD out of Victoria University – with an accompanying exhibition – that examines Duchamp's influence on New Zealand artists. (20) As an artist active in the 1970s, I appear in the PhD and am represented at Adam Gallery at Victoria University. However, and maybe ironically, I accepted inclusion in the thesis only on the proviso Duchamp did not influence directly my art works of the time. Instead, I acknowledge I was a voracious student of his work and writings just when significant tomes on his complete oeuvre were beginning to appear in the 60s and 70s. (21) At one time, I withdrew my work from the Adam Gallery show because the PhD graduate did not resist examiners' demands to align Duchamp with a 1960's artistic movement, so obliging the graduate to conform to the Tertiary conception of creativity against the evidence (pers comm).

All the artists in the exhibition draw on secondary themes peripheral to Duchamp's principal focus on the logic of mythic expression. (22) They are influenced by issues such as chance, movement, optical phenomenon, mechanics, transparency, puns, which Duchamp used directly or themes such as nominalism and alchemy, which Duchamp refers to very obliquely or unintentionally. (23) My interest is in Duchamp's major works and their role in providing the overarching philosophic basis for all his other works.

Significantly, Duchamp does something with his complete body of work no other modern artist comes anywhere near achieving. In his early major work *The Bride Stripped Bare by Her Bachelors, Even* (aka the *Large Glass* – 1913-23), Duchamp lays out the logical conditions for any mythic expression. (24) As satellites to the *Large Glass*, all his other works or *readymades* are based in the same mythic sensibility. To emphasise the significance of the *Large Glass* as the generating statement for everything else he made, Duchamp parenthesised his whole oeuvre with a counterpointing final major work *Etant donnes*, which was unveiled only after he died in 1968. *Etant donnes* recapitulates in figurative form exactly the same content as the schematic *Large Glass*.

Octavio Paz the Mexican poet and thinker put it this way: Duchamp effectively makes a 'criticism of myth' by articulating the 'Myth of Criticism'. (25) Paz appreciates that unlike other artists and writers who attempt to incorporate all myths in their works (James Joyce called his multi-mythic writing, 'monomyth' (26)) Duchamp depicts in the *Large Glass* the underlying logic for any mythic expression. Unfortunately, though, when Paz goes on to compare the iconography of the *Large Glass* with Hindu mythology, he slips back into the sensibility that has ruled Tertiary understanding for over a thousand years. (27)

The problem Duchamp resolves goes back to the beginning of scribal culture. His articulation of the logic of any mythic expression, with mythic expression as deepest form of creativity in a culture, corrects 4000 years of male-based mythology by recovering at the level of myth the natural originary status of the female over the male. The implication of his work is that for 4000 years mythic expression has been at odds with reality. Over the last 1000 years particularly, the University as an institution based in the biblical myth (or in failed attempts to shake off the biblical myth as with Nietzsche) has been constrained by adherence in some form to the male-based nature-occluding biblical paradigm.

It is not inconsistent that the heightened ecclesiastical creativity of the period from the gothic through the renaissance was a direct consequence of the conformity of the early Tertiary with the biblical myth. (28) But the downside of the universalising of scripted male-based myth, though, was the accompanying culture of mayhem and murder between irreconcilable sects. (29) Even worse, was the demeaning and marginalising of women with frequent witch hunts, arranged marriages and forced confinements in nunneries. The horrendous dysfunction drove the process of questioning the role of religion in a culture.

But the process of rectifying the inversion of female priority in biblical myth was hamstrung by the system of logic practiced by philosophers. By using the formal logic devised by the Greeks conveniently at the time when there was a need to justify the imposition of male-based domination, validity trumped soundness in philosophy. (30) Biblical inconsistencies could not be completely overturned because an embargo was in place with inquisition, banishment or execution exacted for heresy against challenging its most fundamental tenet – the mind-based nature-creating status of the male God.

Moreover, Duchamp's most revealing insight into the logic of mythic expression is that protagonists in all mythologies reproduce erotically not sexually. (31) This means that every myth of origins – including Genesis and the Christ myth – self-identifies as non-sexual or logically non-biological or as an expression of purely mind-based desire. Through its constitutional eroticism, myth reflexively demonstrates its status as a deeply affective mind-derived story about a period of prehistory we cannot know about. Even modern scientists exhibit the logic of eroticism when they stretch their understanding into Black Holes, Big Bangs and God Particles. (32)

Because no recognised philosopher or scientist in history accommodates the eroticism endemic to mythic expression, the nature-based logic of all life and understanding has never been completely formulated. (33) Only Duchamp in modern times lays out a substantive and systematic understanding of the logic of myth for artistic expression.

The contributions of Darwin and Wittgenstein

It helps at this point to turn to Charles Darwin's *The Descent of Man and Selection in Relation to Sex*. In *The Descent*, Darwin presents his understanding that the mind is a natural consequence of the evolution of the body over evolutionary time. (34) He demonstrates by evidence and argument that the mind-based syndrome of prioritising biblical myth over nature is a construct inconsistent with the natural evolution of the mind from the body in nature. In *The Descent*, he even spends two-thirds of its length examining the erotics of sexual selection in animals. (35) He, though, was too focused on his scientific findings to extend the criticism to human creativity evident in biblical and other myths.

In the annals of modern philosophy, Ludwig Wittgenstein is the foremost philosopher to investigate systematically the natural relationship of the body or world and the human mind without recourse to apologetics. (36) Wittgenstein appreciates that philosophy presents the logic of the world (body) to mind relationship, whereas apologetics is embattled in the psychology of mind constructs.

In his early *Tractatus*, Wittgenstein gets it wrong. He tries to relate body and mind by using a mind-based construct – the atoms and molecules of theoretical physics. (37) His shift from the macrocosm of the extraterrestrial God to the microcosm of atomic physics still fails to provide the appropriate degree of logical multiplicity between language and the world.

In Wittgenstein's second period of philosophy he corrects the mistake and comes to see that 'nature' and 'parents' at the level of ordinary language usage are the unquestioned givens or preconditions behind every kind of language game and are constitutional of what he calls 'forms of life'. (38) However, as Wittgenstein did not analyse the language of art at the mythic level, his investigations fall short of revealing the basis of deep human creativity.

The limitations of Tertiary

Despite the incisive insights of Duchamp, Darwin and Wittgenstein, to my mind, these three seminal thinkers hang rather loosely and could not be said to provide the necessary substance and systematicity to supplant the Tertiary program. This is despite not one of them being studied in sufficient depth in Tertiary. Symptomatic is the focus by the world's artists – including those in New Zealand – on Duchamp's *readymades* without addressing issues raised by the *Large Glass*. (39)

Similarly, the focus on the prehuman in *The Origin of Species* rather than the human in *The Descent of Man* by star scientists such as Richard Dawkins and David Attenborough (40) means humankind is evaluated by the criteria of the Tertiary Geological period of 30 million years ago instead of the current Quaternary period of human evolution. Moreover, the difficulty of seeing the implications of the later Wittgenstein's roughly sketched theory of nature-based language has prevented Tertiary from getting a handle on Shakespeare's global philosophy. (41)

Only after applying for a number of years the breakthrough discovery into Shakespeare's *Sonnet* philosophy was it possible to formulate the above comments on Duchamp, Darwin and Wittgenstein. Shakespeare anticipates and overarches their specialised contributions with a consistency and comprehensiveness that is breathtaking. Only the work of Shakespeare can be said truly to have the required level of substance and systematicity to engender a level of education above Tertiary – which I call the Quaternary.

The breakthrough into Shakespeare's nature-based philosophy

My current work in Shakespeare began in 1995 after I attended by chance a reading of Shakespeare's 154 sonnets. During the reading over a couple of days of the 'love' sonnets (overly romanticised by Tertiary minds), I apprehended a sound and systematic presentation of a philosophy I had cobbled together rudimentarily from my then understanding of the above three thinkers. (42)

Effectively, I can now show, and do show in my writings, that in the set of 154 sonnets Shakespeare publishes in 1609, he articulates a nature-based philosophy that recognises the originary status of the female to the male. Moreover, it accepts the logic of perpetuation or increase we know as Darwinian evolution. It recovers the natural relationship of body before mind, and acknowledges the erotic logic of any mythic expression while giving the natural logic of body and mind a comprehensive and consistent philosophic and artistic expression.

Shakespeare is also devastatingly precise in his understanding of the relationship between incoming sensations from the primary senses and the argumentative logic of language. Even more significant for creativity is his understanding of the move from the give and take that is the lexicon of language to the sensations we generate that are peculiar to our minds as intuitions, art, music and poetry. These are the mind-based sensations to which we give so much value and which have their deepest creative expression in myth.

As apparent in the *Nature template* (below) I derive from the 154 sonnets, Shakespeare lays out an isomorphic connectivity between the sexual dynamic of female and male in nature and the workings of the human mind in terms of sensations, language and art. He fulfils Wittgenstein's hope of finding the correct logical multiplicity between the world and language, illustrates Darwin's arguments about the derivation of mind from

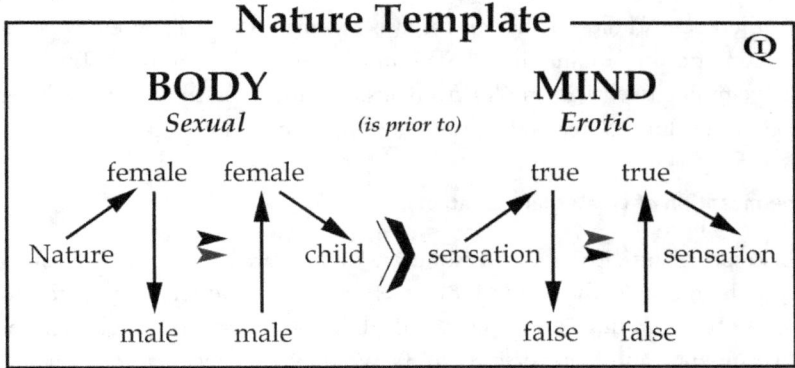

body over evolutionary time and deepens Duchamp's elegant expression of the logic of myth. (43)

In addition, and of no small significance, I show Shakespeare publishes purposefully the *Sonnet* philosophy in 1609 twenty years after he starts writing plays to present the philosophy behind all his plays and longer poems. The *Sonnets* have the same relationship to Shakespeare's plays and poems as Duchamp's *Large Glass* has to his *readymades*. Only Shakespeare and Duchamp in any culture worldwide create a specific work to both articulate the logical conditions for any mythic expression and contextualise their whole oeuvre with that work. The *Sonnets* and the *Large Glass* are unique and at the crux of the blind spot in Tertiary creativity. (44)

We may be beginning to see why no one in 400 years has come anywhere near revealing the *Sonnet* philosophy. More pertinent, is its relevance for a global constituency that is becoming increasingly aware of the harm that the inappropriate application of illogical myths to the body politic have done to nature.

Effectively, since the Enlightenment, Tertiary has been missing its head and in the 3000 years before the Enlightenment its head thought far too much of itself to the point of murder and mayhem to prove one mind-based construct of the male-God had ascendency over the other. We still see the totally avoidable mindless killing in the world today where male-based mind-based constructs battle for ascendency with no recourse to nature and the female as moderating influences. (45)

Significantly, in the *Folio* of 1623, fourteen female-based Comedies are followed by ten male-based Histories and twelve male-based Tragedies. (46) In the *Folio* plays, Shakespeare first shows with his eleven female and three gender-balanced male led Comedies how to correct male-based excesses. He then case studies in the ten English Histories the malconsequences of investing power of Church and State in a Monarchy. Then in the Tragedies he examines twelve examples from history and literature of male-based excesses leading to needless murder and mayhem of kith and kin. (47)

The inception of Quaternary creativity

Shakespeare anticipates the dissolution of Monarchies, the separation of Church and State, the abandonment of patriarchy, the recovery of female rights, the banning of slavery, and the democracy of freely chosen governments and partnerships. (48) We now accept that the natural resolution of these concerns provides the basis of a modern liberal society.

By any measure, Shakespeare bestrides the centuries since then but as yet his nature-based philosophy has not been recognised either in the world about or in educational institutions. Tertiary's inability to appreciate the philosophy embedded in the 154 sonnets and plays is an indictment of its post-modern malaise where it has been unable to break free to be a learning institution of truly global investigation, responsibility and creativity.

The experience of presenting the findings over the first five or so years after 1995, led me in 2000 to create an uncluttered space to continue to unravel the findings with their great explanatory power and global implications. I established the Quaternary Institute for my own peace of mind not quite sure whether Tertiary could be altered to accommodate the discoveries or whether a completely new level of education is required for which Primary, Secondary and Tertiary are the precursors.

When it comes to creativity, or better, a context in which a creative institution can flourish, Duchamp has demonstrated his credentials for art, Darwin for science and Wittgenstein for philosophy. Invention and inventiveness are at the core of evolving humankind as the changing demographics continually challenge us to produce ever-new ways to survive and enjoy.

However, as well as and alongside creativity, Shakespeare in his famous love sonnets and throughout his plays teaches us to mature our natural understanding and experience of love and life. (49) Not only does Shakespeare offer the germ of a substantial and systematic educational creativity, in the process he keeps alive the very qualities of creativity and emotion many find missing from the current Tertiary program. The adolescent male-based love offered by the University from its founding days in Christian Europe has proved inadequate for the demographics of our modern world.

I ask then, is Tertiary or Quaternary the most likely forum where these manifold issues can be addressed and fostered for a learning demographic hungry for ways to embrace nature and ourselves in equal measure. I would participate in a forum that considered the Tertiary/Quaternary hiatus.

Notes:

1. Disquiet about the role of the University appears quite frequently in the media. In a book review titled 'Troubled halls', the *Economist* (February 4th 2012, p 69) considers Stefan Collini's reference in *What Are Universities For* to Newman's expectation that a liberal education might enhance the 'perspective they have on the place of their knowledge in a wider map of human understanding'. What, the reviewer asks, is the relationship between 'intellectual purity' and the 'grubby business of picking and preparing the future middle class?'

2. Around the same time, the *NZ Listener* (March 3rd 2012) features Alain De Botton questioning the relevance of the University to the needs of modern students. Unfortunately, De Botton's very simplistic take on philosophy sees him suggesting the removal of courses on history and literature and replacing them with life-skill programs.

3. Lytton Strachey predicted in 1905 that 'for its solution (the mystery of the *Sonnets*) seem to offer hopes of a prize of extraordinary value – nothing less than a true insight into the most secret recesses of the thoughts and feelings of perhaps the greatest man who ever lived'. *From:* Peter Jones, *Shakespeare Casebook,* London, Macmillan, 1977.

4. Typical is the return to the 1623 *Folio* by the *Original Shakespeare Company* in the early 2000s. They presented their performances entirely from an unedited, unaltered *Folio* text.

5. To mark the 400th anniversary of the publication of the 1609 *Sonnets*, all Shakespeare's plays were performed at Stratford Upon Avon in that year. Despite the recognition accorded the 1609 *Sonnets* in 2009, none of the productions looked to the *Sonnet* philosophy for guidance. This is not surprising as The Shakespeare Institute based in Stratford Upon Avon is an offshoot of Birmingham University, hence Tertiary standards of creativity prevail at the Royal Shakespeare Company. This is evident in the recent *William Shakespeare Complete Works*, Modern Library, 2007,

London, edited by Jonathan Bate, Eric Rasmussen for RSC, which leaves out *A Lover's Complaint* Shakespeare publishes alongside the *Sonnets* but trumpets an anonymous ditty titled *To the Queen*.

6. At the New Zealand International Arts Festival, 2012, there were performances of *Henry V*, *The Winter's Tale* and a Maori-language version of *Troilus and Cressida*. Two independent productions focused on Hamlet's words 'To be, or not to be', and Germaine Greer gave a talk on her book *Shakespeare's Wife*.

7. Roger Peters, *William Shakespeare's Sonnet Philosophy*, Quaternary Imprint, 2005, Kaponga. The Quaternary Institute website is at: *www.quaternaryinstitute.com*. Forthcoming are: *Nature, Love and Shakespeare*, an updated 350-page summary of the 1760 four-volume *WSSP*, a 100-page essay *shakespeare @ love . nature* on mature Shakespearean love, and a *Pictorial Volume* with numerous charts and diagrams as teaching aids for Quaternary. [Editorial note: the three Volumes are now published as *Shakespeare's Global Philosophy* (2017), *Shakespeare & Mature Love* (2018) and *Shakespeare's Philosophy Illustrated* (2019).]

8. This seems to be a common perception of the role of the early University as witnessed by an anecdotal entry online: "…a community of scholars, primarily communicating in Latin, accelerated the process and practice of attempting to reconcile the thoughts of Greek antiquity, and especially ideas related to understanding the natural world, with those of the church. The efforts of this "scholasticism" were focused on applying Aristotelian logic and thoughts about natural processes to biblical passages and attempting to prove the viability of those passages through reason. This became the primary mission of lecturers, and the expectation of students". (From *Wikipedia* entry under 'University'.)

9. Thomas Aquinas drew a distinction between truth available through reason (natural revelation) and faith (supernatural revelation). (Thomas Aquinas, *Summa Theologica*, 1665-73 and *Summa Contra Gentiles*, 1661-3.)

10. Benedict de Spinoza considered God and Nature, or "Deus sive Natura", as having indeterminable attributes. He held that there is no difference between body and mind. (Benedict de Spinoza, *Ethics*, 1677.)

11. Even Ludwig Wittgenstein, despite his determination to avoid traditional metaphysics or apologetics, could not accept the full implications of Darwinian evolution. In a conversation with Maurice Drury, Wittgenstein averred: "I have always thought that Darwin was wrong: his theory doesn't account for all this variety of species (in the Zoological Gardens, Dublin). It hasn't the necessary multiplicity. Nowadays some people are fond of saying that at last evolution has produced a species that is able to understand the whole process which gave it birth. Now that you can't say!" M. O'C. Drury, 'Conversations with Wittgenstein', in *Ludwig Wittgenstein, Personal Recollections*, ed R. Rhees, New York, Rowman and Littlefield, 1981, p. 160.

12. Dean Peter Beck of Christchurch Cathedral, in an interview on TVNZ One, *Closeup*, with Mark Sainsbury after the special commemoration service held in Christchurch's Hagley Park in March 2011. He later reiterated with National Radio's Noelle McCarthy on Sunday, July 3 that God is in the actions of people, in our reaching out to other people, in our being human, and that that love is the lifeblood of the universe (paraphrase).

13. Once the philosophy Shakespeare articulates in his *Sonnets* is understood then the 300 year practice of altering his works to conform with the default Tertiary paradigm is rendered redundant. Shakespeare's *Sonnets*, plays and longer poems make complete sense as published in the early seventeenth century by him and his colleagues. The modern desperation by Mac Jackson of the University of Auckland to justify the emendations made originally by Reverend Malone in the 1790s is a measure of Tertiary frustration. Moreover, the reattribution of parts of plays to other authors by Gary Taylor, as with his recent publishing of parts of *Measure for Measure* in a volume of Thomas Middleton's plays, is a gross admission of failure to work out the philosophy behind Shakespeare's oeuvre.

14. Nietzsche proclaimed the death of the male God of Christianity in his *Gay Science* in 1882.

15. *The Oxford Companion to Philosophy* reports Hume as saying: 'Most fortunately it happens, that since reason is incapable of dispelling these clouds, nature herself suffices to that purpose'. It seemed to Hume that, 'A few hours of good company and backgammon make his melancholy and sceptical conclusions seem ridiculous'. *The Oxford Companion to Philosophy*, p379, Oxford University Press, 1995.

16. Nietzsche says of Shakespeare, "We are all afraid in the face of Truth; and while I recognise that I am instinctively certain and sure of this, that Lord Bacon is the creator, the self-torturer of this most gloomy sort of literature". Alfred von Weber Ebenhof, *Bacon (Shakespeare) and Friedrich Nietzsche*, www.sirbacon.org/nietzsche.htm, accessed 22.06.04.

17. The circularity of the Post-modern or Post-structuralist embargo on meta-theories or meta-figures is warranted for those beliefs and thinkers who demonstrably base their thinking in mind-based constructs as do all biblical religions and the sceptical backlash. Caught in the embargo are thinkers like Darwin, Duchamp and Shakespeare who ground their understanding on preconditions or givens based in nature and the sexual dynamic of female and male, which even Wittgenstein came to appreciate are the undeniable basis of all thinking.

18. See the essay on Duchamp's relationship to Shakespeare in Part 1 of Volume Four of *William Shakespeare's Sonnet Philosophy*.

19. In *Marcel Duchamp or the Castle of Purity* of 1970, Octavio Paz compares Pablo Picasso and Marcel Duchamp characterising Picasso as rendering the century 'visible' and Duchamp as showing that the arts begin and end in the 'invisible' (unpaginated). In what follows we will see the adequacy and inadequacy of Paz's view of Duchamp.

20. Marcus T. G. Moore, *Marcel Duchamp and New Zealand Art, 1965-2007*, PhD Thesis, Victoria University, 2012.

21. For instance, books by Arturo Schwarz not only gave as full a catalogue raisonné as was possible at the time of publishing, they also made available in facsimile form the *Notes* Duchamp published at intervals over his lifetime that explained amongst other things the workings of the *Large Glass*.

22. Calvin Tomkins in his *Marcel Duchamp* of 1998, discusses the influence of Duchamp's readymades on the artists of the 1950s to the 1990s, but near the end of the book Tomkins admits he has not accounted for the *Large Glass* and, frustrated, wonders if it will be necessary to turn to Christian mythology to begin to understand it. (Calvin Tomkins, *Marcel Duchamp*, New York, Owl Books, 1998, p. 465.)

23. Thierry de Duve wrote *Pictorial Nominalism* in 1991 to validate the conceptual artists of the 1960s and 1970s. The issue of Nominalism and the conceptual artists' response to Duchamp's achievement is so peripheral to the mythic logic of the *Large Glass*, de Duve has to devise a theory that the *Large Glass* was an inconsequential joke whose sole purpose was to dismiss the history of art. Nothing could have been further from Duchamp's intent. (Thierry de Duve, *Pictorial Nominalism: On Marcel Duchamp's Passage from Painting to the Readymade*, University of Minnesota Press, 1991.)

24. It is necessary to approach the *Large Glass* knowing that Duchamp published the *Notes* at intervals over his lifetime to provide essential clues to its workings and purpose.

25. Octavio Paz, (unpaginated), toward the end of his short book, comments about 'critical myth' and 'Myth of Criticism'. Paz suggests Duchamp creates a critical myth for the modern age different from 'a professor who makes a criticism of myth'.

26. James Joyce uses the word 'monomyth' in *Finnegan's Wake* into which he packs elements of all the world's myths producing a concatenation of sub-mythic unreadability. In a similar vein, Carl Jung scoured the world's many mythic cultures for their common symbolisms. Joseph Campbell, taking Joyce's lead, talked of

'monomyth' as the ultimate expression of the mythic sensibility. None of them, though, matches Duchamp's penetration of the logic of mythic expression consistent with natural prerogatives.

27. Hindu, Christian and other myths of the world's cultures, as male-based myths, do not have the generic basis to provide the logic of mythic expression.

28. The male or masculine disposition toward idealism, especially when it alienates the originary disposition of the female, produces an intensified creativity that drives the artistic program toward ever more fanciful expressions of otherworldly expectations.

29. The imbalance and prejudice toward women in male-dominant cultures leads to unconscionable misogynistic violence in their societi

30. Demonstrations of validity do no more than connect mind-based constructs in an endless debate as witnessed in the to and fro of philosophical movements over the last 3000 years.

31. Demonstrations of validity do no more than connect mind-based constructs in an endless debate as witnessed in the to and fro of philosophical movements over the last 3000 years.

32. No myth of origins has its principal protagonists reproducing sexually. Mythic births occur from the head, from the thigh, from virgins, from the blood of testicles, from clay, from the rib of the male, etc.

33. Theism and atheism, as Duchamp realised, are flipsides of the same mind-based constructs. He was interested in another possibility. When asked if he believed in God, he replied: 'No, not at all..... God is a human invention.... I don't mean that I'm neither atheist nor believer....'. (Pierre Cabanne, *Dialogues with Marcel Duchamp*, Da Capo, 1971, New York, pp 106-7.)

34. Kant's 'space/time', Schopenhauer's 'Will', Descartes' 'doubt', Wittgenstein's early 'atoms/molecules', all talk to an unwillingness to accept female and male as the logical basis for understanding

and consequently for the eroticism of all expression because no form of understanding can substitute for biological sex. Ironically, all thinkers who avoid the female/male basis for thought adhere to the overarching male/female dynamic in biblical or other myths.

35. In Chapter 3 titled 'Mental Powers' of *The Descent of Man* Darwin says; 'My object in this chapter is to shew that there is no fundamental difference between man and the higher mammals in their mental abilities' p99. He concludes at the end of Chapter 4, which continues the discussion of 'Mental Powers' into 'Moral Sense', by saying; 'Nevertheless the difference in mind between man and the higher animals, great as it is, certainly is one of degree and not of kind' p193. Charles Darwin, *The Descent of Man and Selection in Relation to Sex*, John Murray 1909, London.

36. Part 1 of *The Descent of Man and Selection in Relation to Sex* deals with 'mental powers' and 'moral sense'. Parts 2 and 3, oddly to some, seem to spend an inordinate number of pages on a peripheral topic. However, Darwin recognises that the erotic or secondary sexual characteristics are an important consequence of the separation of male from female over evolutionary time.

37. Following the example of Bertrand Russell and A. N. Whitehead, Wittgenstein takes the atomic world to its logical end point and consequentially demonstrates its inadequacy as a model for logical multiplicity between language and the world.

38. In Proposition 6.53 of his *Tractatus*, Wittgenstein says: 'The correct method in philosophy would really be the following: to say nothing except what can be said, i.e. propositions of natural science – i.e. something that has nothing to do with philosophy – and then, whenever someone else wanted to say something metaphysical, to demonstrate to him that he had failed to give a meaning to certain signs in his propositions'. (Ludwig Wittgenstein, *Tractatus Logico-Philosophicus*, Trans. D. F. Pears and B. F. McGuiness, Routledge and Kegan Paul, 1961, London.)

39. 'Forms of life' are socially determined groupings of language activities that create a sense of connectivity and boundedness for

language users. Because they are effectively constructs, they stand in a secondary relationship to 'nature' or 'parents' or 'natural history' as the grounds or givens for all languages.

40. See Notes 20 to 25 above.

41. Richard Dawkin's theory of 'genes and memes', and the extreme anthropomorphism in his coinage 'selfish genes', applies *Origin of Species* findings to humans. David Loye shows that the *Descent of Man* is where Darwin discusses morals and love – each word occurring over ninety times compared to two times for the survival of the fittest. (David Loye, *Darwin's Lost Theory of Love*, Lincoln, toExcel, 2000.)

42. Like Darwin and Duchamp, Wittgenstein has been reduced methodically to the level of teachability in Tertiary. His challenge to postmodern circularity based in mind-based constructs has largely been ignored.

43. Unpublished booklet, Roger Peters, *Human Being*, 1987.

44. By arguing for nature/female/male/increase as the logical givens for 'truth and beauty' Shakespeare recognises that the mind derives from those preconditions and operates according to their logic – as per the *Nature template*.

45. The relationship of Dante's *La Vita Nuova* to *The Divine Comedy* and the vague reflexivity in the sonnet sequences of Phillip Sidney etc., do not prepare for the massive shift from their psychological romanticism and idealism to the relentless logic of the 1609 *Sonnets*. Similarly, the Cubists, Futurists, etc., do not prepare for Duchamp's *Large Glass* conceived when rejected by his brothers and others because he would not conform to their stylistic/formalistic precepts.

46. Amongst the numerous examples are the religious conflicts between the Palestinians and Israelis, the sectarian feuding in Iraq, Ireland, Sudan etc.

47. In *Shakespeare's Wife*, Germaine Greer argues that Anne Hathaway,

who died in 1623, may have had a part to play in the arrangement of the *Folio* published in 1623 by Shakespeare's close colleagues. Sonnet 145, which seems to pun on Anne Hathaway's name, identifies her as central to his creativity. (Germaine Greer, *Shakespeare's Wife*, London, Bloomsbury, 2007)

48. All the Comedies in the 1623 *Folio* have generic titles in that none of them carry the names of characters. In contrast, all the Histories and Tragedies have the names in their titles of the principal perpetrators of male-based mayhem and murder. The fourteen Comedies are examples of the *Sonnet* philosophy applied to affect a resolution of male-led dysfunction. The twenty-two Histories and Tragedies select named males from history and literature who are responsible for exacting male-based injustices and carnage.

49. Shakespeare's play *Henry VIII*, focuses on the first two wives of Henry VIII's murderous reign to highlight the absurdity of male primogeniture and celebrate with the birth of Elizabeth to Anne Boleyn in the last scenes the inevitable surfacing of female priority. Some Tertiary commentators, immensely uncomfortable with the plays patent content, attribute critical passages to John Fletcher. A. R. Humphreys does so with unparalleled disingenuousness: 'If these sardonic references are Shakespeare's, the King becomes a cynic and a hypocrite, and this the play does not at all seem to intend. If they are Fletcher's – and both occur in scenes attributed to him – the explanation is the simple one that, inadequately consulting Shakespeare's intentions, he intruded them from his sense of worldly court gossip and thus confused the rendering of Henry's motives at a time when, one would deduce, Shakespeare meant them to be honest'. (A. R. Humphreys, Introduction, *Henry VIII*, New Penguin Shakespeare, 1971, p20)

50. *shakespeare @ love . nature* (forthcoming) explores the relationship between mature Shakespearean love and life and art as discussed in his *Sonnets* (esp. sonnets 32 and 80) and explored in his plays and longer poems. [See Note 7.]

Criteria for Quaternary

A response to queries from Professor Michael A. Peters

Preamble

The question 'does quaternary exist' is rhetorical because the Quaternary Institute has existed in the world as a natural fact for fifteen years, which is infinitely longer than God or the Big Bang. As purely mind-generated ideas, Goddesses and Gods and Big Bangs have only ever and can only ever be said to exist within the ephemeral musings of the human imagination.

Rather, the question is how best to reach those who are inclined in varying degrees to trust their idealizing imaginations over their verifiable existence in nature. How best to convey to them the significance and potentiality of the quaternary sensibility derived from Shakespeare's previously unknown nature-based philosophy.

When, in 2002, Philip Stokes publishes his coffee-table book *100 Essential Thinkers* (from the early Greeks to the present day – including Michel Foucault, Jaques Derrida, etc.), he omits William Shakespeare from his list of 100 seminal thinkers. Yet, in his short Introduction, he begins by quoting from *Hamlet* and then asserts Shakespeare's character Hamlet epitomises the philosophic aims of the 100 thinkers.

Considering the brief Introduction is all over Shakespeare, the absence of a chapter on Shakespeare shows Stokes is unable to explain philosophically why his 100 thinkers and Hamlet share a common aim. The dramatic irony is that Hamlet is a dupe who does not get Shakespeare's nature-based philosophy – hence why his play is so irredeemably tragic. Effectively, Shakespeare overarches all other philosophers.

Bertrand Russell in his 1946 *Philosophy of Western Civilization* similarly fails to give Shakespeare a chapter, yet he gives one to the lesser poet Lord Byron. However, not only does Russell mention both 'Nature' and 'Hamlet' on the first page of his Introduction before other substantive concepts or proper names, throughout the lengthy tome he quotes and references Shakespeare and his plays a dozen or so times.

Many philosophers and others have tried but failed to account for Shakespeare's philosophy. Books have been published anthologising the numerous attempts to plumb Shakespeare's thought from Samuel Taylor Coleridge to Friedrich Nietzsche, from Samuel Johnson to T. S. Eliot (note…). Recently Colin McGinn publishes *Shakespeare's Philosophy* (2007) but only considers a handful of plays from the disadvantage of a few traditional psychological/philosophical tropes such as 'cause' and 'self'.

The claim highlighted here is that since 2000 the Quaternary Institute is the only investigative and pedagogic institute worldwide based on the consistent and comprehensive nature-based philosophy Shakespeare presents in his 1609 *Sonnets* – revealed for the first time over the last twenty years. The extraordinary explanatory power of the *Sonnet* philosophy enables a full Quaternary teaching program across all subjects.

However, to qualify as a Quaternary level of education beyond anything available anywhere worldwide in Tertiary, Quaternary needs to meet exacting criteria both as a substantive philosophic advance on Tertiary and by presenting a comprehensive pedagogic program.

From Primary to Quaternary

The Quaternary level of education is a systematic advance in learning beyond the current pedagogic progression through Primary to Secondary to Tertiary – and hence on to Quaternary.

1. While the word Quaternary, like Tertiary, can refer to a geological period, the educational usage simply designates a fourth level of pedagogy beyond the whole of Tertiary worldwide.

2. Post-graduate study or research at the Institute for Advanced Study, Princeton (or other such Institutes), is resolutely Tertiary if it is not contextualized by the Quaternary Criteria outlined below.

3. As only one Quaternary Institute of advanced education exists worldwide, and as it is not yet a formally constituted institution, postulating a Quinary (sic) level of education is only of academic interest.

4. If there was to be a Quinary level of education it would not involve human mind-derived constructs like social machines as they are Tertiary in origin and ends.

5. In effect, as will be seen, the Quaternary level of education rounds out the natural cycle of pedagogic learning and endeavor that begins at birth.

The context for Primary to Tertiary

A child is born with very rudimentary propensities for learning and expression, which quickly develop as she or he is exposed to a plethora of mind-based constructs that become formalized in the educational levels of Primary, Secondary and Tertiary.

1. Primary provides education in literacy and numeracy and elementary forms of expression. Primary usually presumes on the default mythology in the particular culture.

2. Secondary imparts basic ideas in literature and science and artisti- expression. Secondary similarly presumes on the parent myth with an awareness of other mythologies.

3. Tertiary encourages the development of sophisticated constructs across a wide range of disciplines. Tertiary considers multiple mythologies albeit with the default myth of the culture surfacing in graduation ceremonies. (In New Zealand, the default mythology is the male-based biblical sect of Henry VIII's Anglican Church.

Criteria for Quaternary

The Quaternary level of education reasserts the natural dynamic inherent in the neonate and, within a nature-based philosophical context, rectifies and recontextualises the male-based mind-based constructs developed from Primary to Tertiary with their inculcated inconsistencies and illogicalities.

1. The natural logic of Quaternary pedagogy provides a context for

all the disciplines taught and researched in Tertiary and redirects their accomplishments into globally beneficial practices.

2. Quaternary shows how mind-based constructs like God and the Big Bang are the consequence of an over-reliance on apologetic validity in philosophy, theoretical over-dependence in science, and purely mind-based inventions like zero and infinity in mathematics.

3. Quaternary exposes the prejudicial and unjust imposition of male-based mythologies and cultures that deny and denigrate the natural originary status of the female as the progenitor for the male.

4. Quaternary involves applying the logic of all mythic expression to understand and ameliorate the benefits and malconsequences of mind-based male-based mythologies.

5. Quaternary has implications for a global constituency across all areas of political, social and cultural expression and activities. It holds accountable before nature the excesses of male-based mind-based mythologies, constructs and impositions.

Shakespeare as the first and only Quaternary philosopher

The works of William Shakespeare provide the only consistent and comprehensive expression and articulation of the Quaternary sensibility. Shakespeare intentionally presents his nature-based female-priority philosophy in the *Sonnets* he publishes in 1609 as the philosophy behind all his plays and poems.

1. The 1609 *Sonnet* set, with precisely 154 sonnets, identifies the word nature as the only generic concept in the English language that is always singular and never associated with an article in ordinary usage.

2. The 154 sonnets recognise, in their division into 28 Mistress sonnets and 126 Master Mistress sonnets, the precursor status of the female and the subsidiary role of the male.

3. The first 14 sonnets take as a given the biological (evolutionary) requirement for humankind to increase if the species is to survive beyond the current generation.

4. Shakespeare's sonnet set correctly considers, and structures into the arrangement of the whole set as consequent on the female/male dynamic of the body, the natural inter-relationship between unmediated incoming senses, the true/false logic of articulate language, and unmediated interior sensations of the mind.

5. Significantly, a dedicated group of five sonnets account for our ability to write about the undeniable givens of nature and the female priority by accepting that writing is conditional on the givens and that the givens make writing and expression possible.

6. The *Sonnets* accept there is a direct relationship between the offshoot status of the male and the capacity of language to create constructs and constructions that are in effect false outside the confines of the human mind and human endeavour. Rather, the male propensity leads directly to the facility to hypothesise for cultural, scientific and other purposes.

7. By laying out the logical components of human life and understanding while accounting for the ability to write poetry that captures the role of myth in any culture, Shakespeare sets down the logical conditions for any mythic expression, which he adheres to in his thirty-six plays in the 1623 *Folio*.

8. Critically, in the 14 increase sonnets that head the set, Shakespeare differentiates between the bodily act of sexual reproduction and eroticism of mind-based desire. As all myths of creation are constitutionally erotic – no Goddess or God in myths of creation reproduces biologically – then all mythologies (and hence all Goddesses and Gods) are desire mechanisms consequent on increase in nature.

The Nature template derived from Shakespeare's Sonnets

From Shakespeare's logical structuring of the 154 sonnets, a *Nature template* can be drawn to show all the above relationships schematically. Shakespeare's nature-based philosophy is the only philosophy capable of representing logically and isomorphically the relationship of body and mind with the body in nature giving rise to the mind (as in Darwinian evolution).

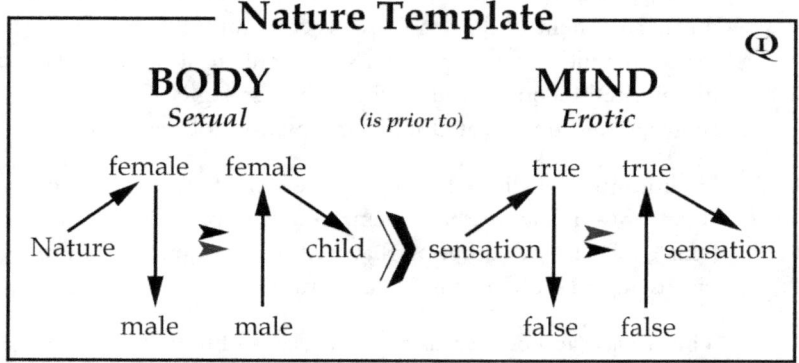

1. The *Nature template* schematises the qualitative and pedagogic difference between Quaternary and the current Tertiary paradigm.

2. Shakespeare's telling achievement, which allows those like Stokes and Russell to sense he overarches all other philosophers, is the arrangement of the 1609 *Sonnets* so that nature and the female/male biology of the body dynamic form the unquestionable givens for the sensory and cognitive functions of the mind. No other so-called philosopher is as rigorous in insisting on the natural relationships.

3. That Shakespeare's *Sonnet* philosophy has remained unknown to Tertiary for 400 years symptomises the excessive dependence of Tertiary on discriminatory mind-based male-based mythologies and constructs.

4. Thinkers like Darwin, Wittgenstein and Duchamp (and many others in various ways) have arrived at an understanding of portions of the *Nature template* while not advancing to describe its complete configuration. That they have not noticed its brilliant expression in the 1609 *Sonnets* indicates significant lacunae in Tertiary expectations attributable to a continued

adherence to aspects of its founding biblical/Platonic paradigm in Medieval Europe (or earlier).

5. The problem for Tertiary – consonant with the current impression it is in its death throes – is not in the depths of its research programs, but is instead philosophic as it doggedly adheres to an inconsistent paradigm.

6. The distinguishing mark of the Quaternary program is its adherence to a completely consistent and comprehensive globally viable paradigm based in nature and female priority isomorphic with the human mind.

7. As with the establishment of Tertiary over 1000 years ago in isolated academes of learning and research, the Quaternary level of pedagogy will begin as stand-alone institutes preparing the way for a wholesale adoption of Quaternary logic over time affecting each level of learning from Primary to Tertiary.

8. The first such Quaternary Institute is sited on the banks of the Kapuni River in South Taranaki, New Zealand.

Why a God template is full of inconsistencies

The problem for Tertiary can be captured by an attempt to reconfigure the *Nature template* as a *God template* to force the *Nature template* to accord with contrived male-based mind-based prerogatives.

1. Although the biblical paradigm represented by the *God template* incorporates all the components of the *Nature template*, it inverts and converts them into an illogical morass of empirical and illogical contradictions. The inability of Tertiary to recognise the extent of the problem, along with its failure to uncover Shakespeare's *Sonnet* philosophy over a period of 400 years, reveals a massive lacunae in its program and provides an explanation for its current malaise.

2. Typically, Postmodernism is symptomatic of Tertiary's failure to break out of the perpetual psychology-as-philosophy syndrome of the last 4000 years into accepting philosophy as philosophy –

a recovery project Wittgenstein begins hesitatingly but only Shakespeare accomplishes magisterially.

3. Perversely, the attempt in the *God template* to mimic natural logic – albeit in reverse – reveals the source of Tertiary's the lack of insight into the metaphysics of mythologies. The ignorance of the relationship between articulate language and the interior sensations of the mind amongst both theologians and scientists leads to the most preposterous postulations of imaginary heavenly entities like God or the Big Bang for an entire universe created from nothing.

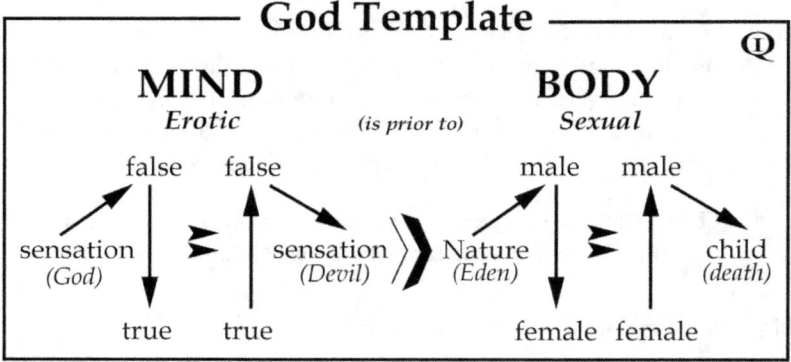

4. However, the purely theoretical postulations based on mathematical 'sense' cannot explain the actual moment of origin because the zero and infinity in mathematics are entirely a mind-based conventions introduced for the purposes of computation so exposing the limitations of Tertiary metaphysics.

5. In the Twentieth Century, Marcel Duchamp resolutely explores and encapsulates the logic of mythic expression by understanding the relationship between articulate language and the interior artistic sensations of all human minds. That his efforts have been ignored not only by scientists and theologians but by artists as well epitomises the tragedy of persisting with Tertiary expectations in the face of his proto-quaternary brilliance.

The explanatory power of Shakespeare's nature-based philosophy

A measure of the success of a seminal insight is its explanatory power. The findings in question need not only account completely for the area of investigation specific to the findings but should be fruitful across a wide range of disciplines. In the case of Shakespeare's nature-based philosophy, as the groundedness for a Quaternary level of advanced education, the explanatory power beyond his own works creates the possibility of an interdisciplinary institution that accommodates all modes of enquiry.

1. It can be shown Shakespeare intentionally arranges his set of 154 sonnets and publishes them in 1609 to present the nature-based philosophy underpinning all human experience, understanding and expression. The philosophy, as discovered twenty years ago, accounts for every aspect of the structuring and numbering of the whole set and all its incidental features.

2. It further follows, and is demonstrated readily, that Shakespeare publishes the *Sonnets* around twenty years after writing his first play to present the philosophy behind all the plays and longer poems. Every aspect of the arrangement and content of the 1623 *Folio* of thirty-six plays is explicable only by applying the *Sonnet* logic.

3. No emendations, reattributions or disparagement of parts, and no authorship issues, etc., which constitute the bulk of Tertiary scholarship on Shakespeare, are required from the vantage of their inherent nature-based philosophy.

4. As indicated in the Preamble, Shakespeare's nature-based philosophy overarches every attempt to formulate a consistent and comprehensive philosophy over the last 4000 or more years. Every philosopher of the period magnifies one or other of the components of the *Nature template* but none incorporates them all into a consistent and comprehensive philosophy as does Shakespeare – and none of them since 1609 have worked out his *Sonnet* logic.

5. Shakespeare's crucial acceptance of the natural female priority and the offshoot status of the male allows his philosophy to avoid the psychological contradictions and prejudices of the founding male-based mind-based biblical paradigm of Tertiary.

6. By showing the logical interconnection between the biologically sexual dynamic of female and male and the feminine and masculine gender dispositions of the mind, the philosophy accounts for the variety of human types without prejudice – as evident in Shakespeare's plays.

Conditions for a Quaternary Level of Education

An advanced teaching and research program is inherent in the overarching status of Shakespeare's nature-based philosophy. Shakespeare and his works already provide a staple – which in some institutions is compulsory – for many Secondary and Tertiary courses, albeit with texts featuring the corrupt editing and commentary generated by Tertiary academics and others over the last 400 years.

1. Because Shakespeare is the only thinker ever to have specifically articulated a consistent and comprehensive nature-based philosophy, his works provide the principal locus around which Quaternary pedagogy devolves over time with the expectation the programs will lead to further expressions of natural logic on a par with or in advance of Shakespeare's contribution.

2. The contributions of proto-Quaternary minds like Darwin, Duchamp, Wittgenstein and a few others enable the over-arching philosophy of Shakespeare to be contextualised by practitioners whose works bring pedagogic variety to the mix.

3. Shakespeare's nature-based philosophy contextualises all forms of scientific and mathematical endeavor as well as articulating the logical conditions for the deepest of all artistic expression, the mythic.

4. Shakespeare's philosophy easily accommodates the complete works of thinkers like Darwin, Mallarmé, Wittgenstein and

Duchamp who, in varying ways, prove resistant to Tertiary exegesis or challenge Tertiary prerogatives. By comparison, artists like Kazimir Malevich are resolutely Tertiary in their expectations.

5. Because of the range of political, social and religious concerns Shakespeare addresses in his plays, their native philosophy provides the basis for a new approach to the disciplines deriving from those studies.

Summary of findings and implications

The discovery and articulation of Shakespeare's nature-based philosophy from his 1609 *Sonnets* as the basis for a Quaternary level of advanced pedagogy is a fiat accompli. The question is not 'does Quaternary exist' but, as Thomas Kuhn anticipates clearly, for how long will the current Tertiary paradigm continue to defend the indefensible before succumbing to the inevitable.

Concomitant with understanding Shakespeare's brilliant philosophy is the acceptance it will take time to bring a truly global understanding and sensibility into the light of day as a fully constituted pedagogic opportunity. Because of Shakespeare's awareness of global sensibilities – witness his involvement in the renaming of the Globe Theatre not long after the circumnavigation of the planet – the Quaternary pedagogy based on his insights restores humankind to its natural roots whilst acknowledging all the specialised advancements in science and art achieved throughout the Tertiary enterprise.

The Quaternary philosophy gives substance and energy to the bare precepts of the Charter of the United Nations, where all states gather free from any particular mythology. Rather than dwelling on doomsday eschatological scenarios, there is now an opportunity to embrace a forward looking philosophical connectivity that both accommodates the highest levels of intellectual excellence and carries with it an appreciation of the most mature love humankind can experience – which is the achievement of Shakespeare's *Sonnets*.

Roger Peters May 2015

Quaternary Pedagogy

Toward a Quaternary level of education

The Quaternary level of understanding and expression, embracing as it does the previously undiscovered philosophy of William Shakespeare, requires a new method of teaching and learning commensurate with its unique philosophic consistency and comprehensiveness. Over the next few years, the Quaternary Institute will seek ways to impart its findings in keeping with the pedagogic standards set by its principal protagonist Shakespeare and the few other proto-Quaternary thinkers.

Foremost in the Quaternary program are Shakespeare's 1609 *Sonnets*, his 1623 *Folio* of thirty-six plays and his four longer poems. His works already perform a teaching/learning role as part of the curriculum in both Secondary and Tertiary education, and have done so for many years. Yet, until now, their pedagogic role as vehicles for a nature-based philosophy happens only by default.

If Shakespeare wrote his sonnets, plays and poems to impart his nature-based philosophy, then, their use in educational institutions over the last few centuries transmits the philosophy purely by osmosis. Fortunately, despite extremely prejudicial editing and commentary that imposes by force a contrary paradigm on his works, generations of teachers and students still respond to the natural attractivity of the sonnets, plays and poems.

Shakespeare's works, then, are the first recourse for a Quaternary teaching program. The fourteen Comedies that lead out the plays in the 1623 *Folio*, demonstrate systematically how to anticipate and correct the excesses of male-based idealism. Shakespeare draws on nature as a continual resort to critique the headstrong characters exacting patriarchal prejudice on their subjects.

In the Comedies, Shakespeare allows eleven savvy and cunning females and three gender-balanced males to take charge. In the process, he demonstrates how the characters – and the audience – can imbibe the philosophic content of a deep nature-based/female-based understanding that enables life to be contented through natural equanimity.

Because Shakespeare intentionally publishes the *Sonnets* in the 1609 edition to present the compleat nature-based philosophy, of all his works the 154-sonnet set provides the best practice model for Quaternary pedagogy. He organises the 154 sonnets to represent nature and divides the set into two sequences to represent female and male. The arrangement provides a sound basis for his articulation of the relationship between human understanding and expression. The natural consistency of the principal components of the philosophy prepares the ground for the logical argument and lyrical depth within the set. The consummate effect is to ensure the most mature, fruitful and beneficial learning outcomes ever devised.

To contextualise Shakespeare's overarching philosophic achievement, the Quaternary program will examine the specialised philosophic contributions and pedagogic implications of the scientific writings of Charles Darwin, the anti-metaphysical investigations of Ludwig Wittgenstein, and the art works of Marcel Duchamp. Of interest also are the philosophic/pedagogic consequences of Thomas Jefferson's separation of Church and State in the Declaration of Independence and American Constitution (and evident in his design for Virginia University). It should be instructive to examine the quite distinct approaches of these proto-Quaternary minds to imparting intellectual ideas or accounting for aesthetic effects.

In *The Origin of Species* and *The Descent of Man*, Darwin manages to convey to generations of readers both the detailed evidence for evolution as well as his deeply ethical sensibility. He does so uniquely because he adheres strictly to the investigative technique known as *vera causa*. By extrapolating from the known facts of artificial selection in existing species to the evolutionary development over millions of years in preexisting species years through natural selection, he avoids fruitless speculation on metaphysical theories on origins, etc.

Darwin's combination of deep evidential content and ethical values has some correspondences with the investigative integrity of Wittgenstein's philosophic methods. When teaching in the 1930s and 40s, Wittgenstein's habit is to combine intense thinking about his current philosophic concerns with expostulatory statements to evince unguarded responses. His students witness Wittgenstein in the process of searching for evocative metaphors to convey his thoughts about the logic of ordinary language.

His notions of language games, forms of life, and natural history prove effective in conveying the basic ethos of the way humans use language.

The artist Duchamp demonstrates throughout his aesthetically coherent oeuvre a standard of unwavering integrity in a body of work that speaks volumes to generations of younger artists. Duchamp's refusal to academicise his insights into the deepest level of artistic expression, the mythic, allows him to present an unrelenting picture of the workings of the aesthetic impulse at the deepest level. His continual use of puns and ellipsis aids rather than detracts from the receptivity of his basic ideas.

In revolutionary America, Jefferson legislates to ensure none of the many religious sectarian denominations can take control of the State. Instead, by accepting the world operates according to the 'Laws of Nature', Jefferson recognises that all Churches share an undemocratic tendency to autocratic male-based rule best proscribed from the center of political life.

Because the Tertiary program is doctrinairely selective about what it teaches of these proto-Quaternary thinkers, their complete body of works offer greater depths of understanding than academia permits. The Quaternary program examines the gap to see just how their works manage to convey the deep content and integrity over and above prohibitive Tertiary education methodologies.

Shakespeare's Sonnet philosophy

This essay considers a previously unknown learning opportunity. Only in the light of Shakespeare's *Sonnet* philosophy does it make sense to talk of a Quaternary pedagogy. No other thinker or system of thought offers such a consistent and comprehensive philosophy to justify instituting a completely new level of systematic education beyond Tertiary – the Quaternary.

Not only does no one else in 400 years plumb the depth and breadth of Shakespeare's nature-based philosophy, the failure of Tertiary scholarship to glimpse even a fraction of its natural logic means the uniqueness and depth of the sound philosophy is completely absent from the highest levels of twenty-first century education. This represents a massive systemic failure across Tertiary for a thinker/dramatist/poet of Shakespeare's significance.

I detail Shakespeare's *Sonnet* philosophy, as evident in the 1609 edition, in the four-volume 1760-page set *William Shakespeare's Sonnet Philosophy* (2005/2019). The volumes include a study of the implications of the 1609

Sonnet philosophy for all his plays and poems and an analysis of 400 years of misunderstanding by Tertiary commentators.

There are now also three further volumes. The first is a summary volume, *Shakespeare's Global Philosophy* (2017), which includes fresh insights through the consistent application of the sonnet logic over the last twelve years. The second, *Shakespeare & Mature Love* (2018), is a study of the mature love Shakespeare describes in the 154 sonnets and presents through select characters in his *Folio* of thirty-six plays. The third, *Shakespeare's Philosophy Illustrated* (2019), is a pictorial volume with speech balloon commentaries on the seventy pages of the 1609 edition of the *Sonnets*, charts and diagram illustrating salient aspects of the philosophy and an illustrated set of comments on enigmatic artworks.

It is not possible to appreciate the gap between Tertiary and Quaternary until those unsure of its potential consider and assimilate a substantial amount of the material already published or available on the Quaternary Institute website www.quaternaryinstitute. com. Shakespeare's *Sonnet* philosophy reinstitutes the default status of singular nature over the plethora of imaginary or mind-based Goddesses and Gods. It recovers the biological default of the female as the progenitor of the male. These two simple moves alone correct at the most profound level 4000 years of imposed male-based/mind-based prejudices and Tertiary apologetics.

Shakespeare understands that mind-based ethics and aesthetics – or truth and beauty as he calls them – derive from bodily dispositions in nature with its female/male default. His consistent and comprehensive philosophy avoids the perennial dilemmas or problems that beset traditional philosophy when it inverts and perverts the natural order.

Across Shakespeare's plays, there is a relentless exposé and criticism of the inevitable malconsequences male-based mythologies. Shakespeare examines the disastrous consequences of imposing mind-derived beliefs against natural prerogatives. By recognising the erotic logic of all myths he reveals their status as mind-based stories. Moreover, by recovering the default biology of female partnership with the offshoot male, he writes plays at a mythic level of expression without the imaginary delusions of traditional male-based mythologies.

The *Nature template* I derive from the 154 sonnets lays out the basic components of Shakespeare's philosophy. Shakespeare builds up his consistent and comprehensive logic, which accounts for all possibilities out of the readily observable givens enabling human life in nature.

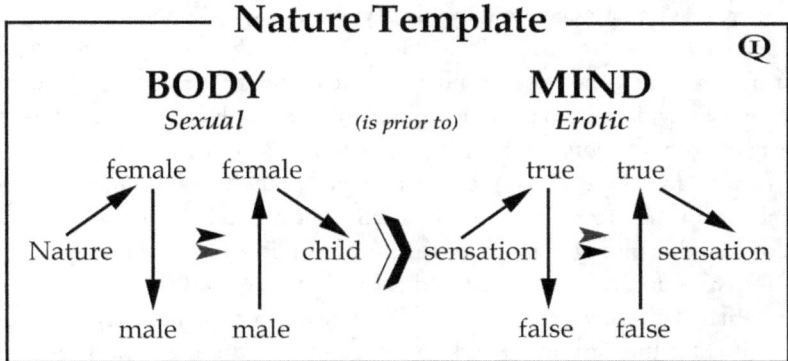

Nature is the only generic word in everyday use without plural and without supplementary definition. All humans derive from the sexual dynamic of female and male in nature and all are the consequence of the dynamic of increase or reproduction. Each human being is conscious of incoming sensations and uses language based on the dynamic of true and false to communicate.

More significantly, for understanding the human imagination, every person experiences the internal sensations of the mind in the form of intuitions, love, religious experience or artistic inspiration. Shakespeare, above all other profound thinkers and poets, is equally conscious he conveys his thoughts and emotions through the medium of poetry.

Shakespeare demonstrates that by adhering to the facts of human life and the natural dispositions of sense and intellect, he is able to account logically for every aspect of human life. Moreover, as the interest in his works over the last 400 years shows, he is able to write the most integrated, engaging and challenging poetry and drama ever penned.

The institution of Tertiary

The Quaternary level of mature education presupposes the continuing viability of the three current levels of age-related learning. The institutionalisation of Primary, Secondary and Tertiary stages of instruction ensures consistent standards of achievement.

Historically, Primary education equates to pre-scribal societies from before 4000 years ago where learning was largely oral. The aim of compulsory Primary education is to teach literacy, numeracy and writing to all pupils. It also begins to establish the basis for developing skills in science, mathematics, geography, history and the social sciences.

Secondary equates to scribal cultures in which writing using linear script is adopted universally and the developments presaged in Primary become a wide-ranging curriculum. However, only over the last sixty years or so has Secondary become mandatory in most countries.

Tertiary, for its part, was once the preserve of the few who matriculated from Secondary to advance academically. Now, like Secondary before it, Tertiary is becoming mandatory for most vocational opportunities.

Tertiary education was instituted formally around 1100AD in Bologna and Paris. The move coincided with renewed interest in classical Greek culture after the cloistering of knowledge during the medieval period or dark ages. Since Tertiary's inception under the auspices of the Catholic Church, it remains predicated on the biblical male-based paradigm.

Shakespeare's nature-based philosophy as the default for Primary, Secondary and Tertiary

Shakespeare's works are an established mainstay of the educational curriculum and are often compulsory for Secondary and Tertiary examination across jurisdictions (as in Britain and the Commonwealth). Largely by default, for teachers and educators they provide the nature-based paradigm that underpins all forms of education at all levels.

Shakespeare's works are mandatory in many Secondary schools as pupils develop their rational and creative potentials. Although Shakespeare may be introduced in Primary using texts such as the Charles and Mary Lamb's incredibly facile *Tales of Shakespeare* and other Shakespeare made simple books, by the time they reach Secondary students are ready to engage with the plays, even directing and staging their own productions. Greater specialisation in Tertiary with more vocation-based courses means not all students study Shakespeare – even those doing humanities courses.

Criminally, though, there is an insidious corruption of the texts used in Secondary and Tertiary through the prejudicial culture of paradigm conversion typical of most Tertiary English departments and endemic at the Stratford Institute at Stratford Upon Avon. Hence, the downside of compulsory Shakespeare in Secondary is that students use texts with emendations, reattributions, authorship issues, etc., in which the interference reflects the determined conversion of Shakespeare's works to the prevailing biblical male-based Tertiary paradigm.

Worse even, are the commentaries provided by the offending academics to justify the unwarranted changes. Students who are provided with Oxford, Cambridge and other Tertiary series featuring commentaries on all the plays unwittingly read the introductory material in which Shakespeare's role in providing the underlying nature-based paradigm is undermined by a prejudiced and supposedly authoritative commentary that converts his work by a thousand cuts to the Tertiary paradigm.

Only when students recognise the 1609 edition of the *Sonnets* as authorial is it possible to begin to appreciate they were intentionally published by Shakespeare to present the philosophy behind all his plays and poems. Consequently, only when students recognise the 1623 *Folio* as authorial, can the process of enlivening the study of all Shakespeare's works begin.

Each play is a pedagogical device deployed specifically by Shakespeare to disseminate his nature-based female-default philosophy. The 1623 *Folio* is arranged to emphasise the pedagogical potential of the successful application of the philosophy in the fourteen Comedies and the disastrous consequences of the abrogation of nature-based logic in the ten Histories and twelve Tragedies.

If students in Secondary – and Tertiary – are made aware of Shakespeare's manifest intentions, then the role of the academic interference can be revealed for the literary crime it is. Currently, because so many in positions of authority in Tertiary are responsible for the literary crimes, the necessary tactic is to institute another level of learning – the Quaternary – in which the ideas can be fostered in a climate conducive to the nature-based philosophy of Shakespeare's works.

Conclusion, the relationship between Tertiary and Quaternary

The need for a Quaternary level of education arises not because of a concern about the state of Tertiary pedagogy. The opposite is the case. After years of study of thinkers considered problematic in Tertiary, I happened on a philosophy completely unknown within Tertiary yet overarching its philosophical paradigm and hence all the philosophers of the last 4000 years or so. The insights not only explain the difficulty posed for Tertiary by those apparently problematic thinkers, it shows that their specialized contributions could be combined to approximate the consistency and comprehensiveness of the newfound philosophy.

With a systematic philosophy of considerable explanatory power available, it soon became apparent not only is it unknown in Tertiary, the Tertiary paradigm is constitutionally too limited to accommodate it. It is necessary, though, to pass through Tertiary pedagogy to begin to access, appreciate and apply the Quaternary philosophy. Hence in 2000, I created a new pedagogic space called Quaternary to explore and prepare the findings for advanced investigation, learning and expression.

The idea William Shakespeare's works are based on a sound and substantive philosophy has long been mooted. Many books and articles have been written either attempting to delineate the philosophy behind all his works or aligning his thinking with traditional or modern schools of philosophy. Both approaches are stymied by adherence in some degree to the founding Tertiary male-based biblical/Platonic paradigm.

The difficulty for Tertiary is in the level of intellectuality and artistry required to broach Shakespeare's brilliant nature-based philosophy written intentionally for a burgeoning global constituency. He knew he was preparing for an age beyond the inconsistencies and injustices in the floundering Tertiary paradigm.

It is necessary to realise Shakespeare intentionally articulated his nature-based philosophy in the 1609 *Sonnets* as the philosophy behind all his plays and that it is only possible to appreciate the philosophy by bringing together the specialised insights of post-Tertiary thinkers like Darwin, Wittgenstein, Mallarme, Duchamp, Jefferson (as I did over the period 1970 to 1995). Only then does the brilliant nature-based philosophy structured precisely into the *Sonnets* become patently clear and applicable.

Shakespeare's *Sonnet* philosophy is the only philosophy ever written capable of justifying the establishment of a Quaternary level of learning wholly beyond current Tertiary education. As with a Secondary student approaching Tertiary for the first time, any Tertiary graduate of whatever station from BA to the most decorated professor faces a quantum jump in expectations and intellectual demands.

The transition from Tertiary to Quaternary is entirely voluntary as befits a mature level of study. The demands of the Quaternary program self-select those most capable or most willing to move from a circumscribed mind-based pedagogy to a global nature-based pedagogy.

Upgrading from Tertiary to Quaternary

Resources for information and advancement

In 2000, I inaugurated the Quaternary Institute to accommodate a fully post-Tertiary level of inquiry and education. The initiative followed the discovery in 1995 of the consistent and comprehensive nature-based philosophy William Shakespeare embeds in his 1609 *Sonnets* as the basis for his 1623 *Folio* of thirty-six plays and his four longer poems.

Now in 2020, the Quaternary Institute can consolidate the process of superseding the apologetic inadequacies of the Tertiary paradigm. As no one has previously plumbed the *Sonnet* philosophy, and as Shakespeare's plays and poems can be understood only from the vantage of the philosophy he articulates in his set of 154 sonnets, then the Quaternary Institute is uniquely placed to offer pedagogic resources to supersede Tertiary limitations.

A Quaternary paradigm for a nature-orientated global constituency

My ability to apprehend the depth and breadth of Shakespearean thought came after years studying the difficulties presented by a few seminal thinkers whose works are not fully conformable with the Tertiary paradigm (see below). Moreover, the unprecedented explanatory power of Shakespeare's *Sonnet* philosophy means it supersedes all other attempts over time to articulate a sound and inclusive philosophy.

Shakespeare's nature-based philosophy demonstrates that all other so-called philosophies are forms of psychological justification or apologetics for the biblical/Platonic (or similar) paradigms. In particular, biblical/Christian mythology underpins the psychological apologia for Tertiary from around 1100AD to the present day.

In keeping with Shakespeare's reputation as a nature Poet and the longstanding recognition he bases his works in nature, his *Sonnet* philosophy takes nature as the unconditional given for all else. Because in everyday language we use the word nature without plural or other provisos, we accept involuntarily nature's status as the singular precondition for everything. In contrast, the words God, universe, world, etc., all have plural forms, or we legislate them into usurpatious singularity over nature.

Shakespeare's 154 sonnets, as he organises them in the edition of 1609, adhere unerringly to natural prerogatives. The whole set of 154 sonnets represents singular nature, while the two sequences of 126 and 28 sonnets within the set represent the male and the female, respectively.

Consistent with the natural preconditions, Shakespeare's philosophy recognises the female as the default for the male. In the biology of sexual dimorphism, the male is an offshoot of the female. As sonnet 20 avers, in 'nature' the male is 'created' for the female. The male needs to return to the female for the perpetuation of humankind or what sonnets 1 to 14 call 'increase'. The increase argument is not that everyone should increase. Rather that if no one increases, as inferred in some male-based beliefs, humankind ceases to exist.

With these three moves – the singularity of nature, the default of female over male and the intractable logic of increase – Shakespeare incorporates a natural basis for a sound philosophy while critiquing simultaneously all other inconsistent mind-based and male-based philosophies before or since. Unless thinkers acknowledge the natural givens, their philosophising is but psychological justification or apologetics.

Once Shakespeare lays out the incontrovertible givens of nature and the female/male default and the implications of increase, he can then articulate the natural logic of the human mind. First, he accounts for incoming sensations whose singular unmediated effects on the mind he calls 'beauty' (sonnets 128 to 137). Then, consequent on incoming sensations within the mind is the swearing and forswearing of true and false that constitutes intelligible language or 'truth' (sonnets 138 to 152).

Then, throughout the male sequence (sonnets 20 to 126), Shakespeare accounts for the mind-derived sensations we refer to as intuitions, ideals, or the sublime (including the epiphanous mind sensation called God). We experience them as singular unmediated sensations – which Shakespeare appropriately also calls 'beauty'.

Shakespeare devotes the majority of the sonnets to this form of beauty, which we give expression to in the arts. He appreciates that these unbidden sensations, generated purely in the mind as a consequence of external sensations inducing language, are a psychological quagmire for susceptible or immature thinkers and poets.

The *Nature template* shows the logical relationships within the 154 sonnets.

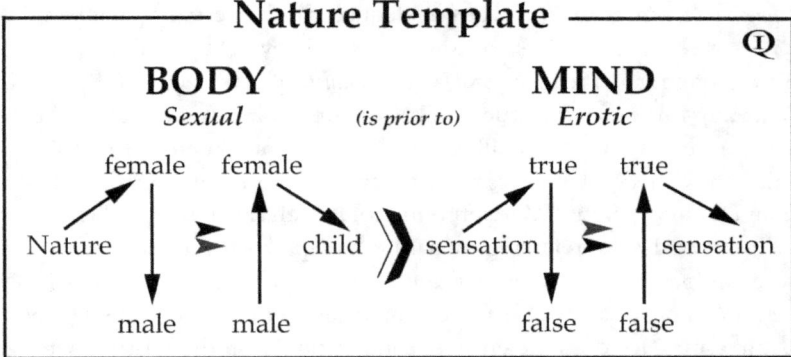

Holding to these natural preconditions, Shakespeare is then able to account for all other characteristics of the mind. Among other issues, he examines the function of writing and particularly the role of the Poet in the set (sonnets 15 to 19), the construct of time, the erotic logic of myths of origin and the relation between natural 'content' and 'contentedness'. In his *Folio* of plays, he applies the insights of natural philosophy to rectify the social, political and religious malconsequences of male-based constructs, such as the Commandments of the Mosaic God with their constitutional usurpation of the female's natural default over the male.

Furthermore, Shakespeare's use of the word 'globe' in his plays (along with the naming of the Globe Theatre in 1598) indicates he was aware his nature-based philosophy, with its genuine mythic level of artistic expression, provides a coherent and inclusive philosophy for a burgeoning global awareness. Shakespeare's increasing popularity over the last fifty years means the recent discovery of the *Sonnet* philosophy, as the basis for his *Folio* of plays, is timely for the twenty-first century with its nature-orientated global constituency.

Reflections on the inadequacy of the historic Tertiary paradigm

The inability of Tertiary scholarship worldwide to penetrate the *Sonnet* philosophy over the last 400 years, combined with the forcible conversion and prejudicial adulteration of Shakespeare's sonnets, plays and poems through editing, emendation and reattribution by academics and others since 1700, points to a grievous inadequacy in the Tertiary paradigm.

An anecdotal measure of the chasm is evident in the entry on Wittgenstein in the *Cambridge Dictionary of Philosophy* (1996). The *Dictionary* makes two crucial observations. First, it doubts whether Wittgenstein's 'thought will ever be fully integrated into academic philosophy'. Second, it notes that by advocating 'a naturalism' or a 'kind of natural human practice' Wittgenstein avoids both absolutism and relativism.

However, despite referring to 'nature' and 'parents' as unassailable givens from the period of the *Philosophical Investigations* to his final notes in *On Certainty*, Wittgenstein does not elaborate a systematic philosophy based in 'naturalism'. Nor does the entry expand critically on the relation between Wittgenstein's 'naturalism' and 'academic philosophy'. Instead, it devotes considerable collegial energy to thinkers such as Foucault and Heidegger, whose academic philosophising is conformable with Tertiary prerogatives.

I identify two other thinkers whose work, like Wittgenstein's, is not integrated fully into Tertiary. Most academics ignore Charles Darwin's *Descent of Man* as the basis for understanding the 'mental powers' and 'moral sense' of humankind. Rather, like Richard Dawkins, they use Darwin's study of precognitive sensibilities in *Origin of Species* to account for the human mind and ethics. Academia similarly does not accommodate the mythic critique and content of Marcel Duchamp's seminal art works *The Large Glass* and *Etant donnes*. It prefers to derive simplistic formalistic devices from his *readymades*.

The doubts raised within Tertiary as to whether academic philosophy will ever fully integrate Wittgenstein's thought is true also of Darwin and Duchamp. Yet, significantly, the aspects of their works currently outside the purview of academia are not subject to denigration and reattribution. While some academics acknowledge the presence of the difficult content, the limited forays by the three thinkers beyond Tertiary precepts makes it possible to ignore their unsystematic insights.

The same cannot be said of Shakespeare. The complete blindness of Tertiary scholarship to Shakespeare's *Sonnet* philosophy over 400 years has led in part to the postmodern malaise and the literary crimes endemic in academia of willful reconfiguration, reattribution or rewriting of Shakespeare's works. Only Shakespeare's complete works are subject to such presumptuous and demeaning treatment.

Although many sense philosophic depths in Shakespeare works, none are sufficiently free of Tertiary proscriptions to appreciate the uncanny scope and incisiveness of Shakespeare's thought and emotions. Bertrand Russell quotes from Shakespeare's works numerous times in his *A History of Western Philosophy* (1946). Yet, while he gives many lesser thinkers/poets such as Byron a chapter, Shakespeare does not qualify for one. Significantly, Shakespeare does not rate one mention in the *Cambridge Dictionary* or the *Oxford Companion to Philosophy* (1995).

Working to remedy the pedagogical deficiencies within Tertiary

Over the last eighteen years, I have investigated exhaustively Shakespeare's nature-based philosophy and its implications. I present extensive evidence and argument in the four-volume 1760-page publication *William Shakespeare's Sonnet Philosophy* (2005), in four forthcoming publications, in correspondence and in postings on the Quaternary Institute website (see below).

In manuscript is a 360-page summary volume *Shakespeare's Global Philosophy* (published 2017), a 100-page monograph *Shakespeare & Mature Love* (published 2018) on mature Shakespearean love and an A4 90-page teaching-aid volume *Shakespeare's Philosophy Illustrated* (published 2019) of charts and diagrams. In preparation, is an A3 910-page volume of speech-balloon commentaries on the text of the 1623 *Folio* of plays. (The last two are also digitalised for data-show screening.)

The conclusion is that only Shakespeare's 'naturalism', which he lays out in the *Sonnet* philosophy, has the required degree of consistency and comprehensiveness to initiate a new level of systematic education free of the Tertiary dichotomy between absolutism and relativism. The combination of the nature-based philosophy Shakespeare articulates in the 154 sonnets and his exploration of its political, social and religious ramifications in the thirty-six plays in the *Folio* and the four longer poems provide the basis for a curriculum that stands entirely beyond current Tertiary strictures and confusion.

Having largely completed the process of investigation into the previously unknown philosophy, I am now developing the material for a Quaternary level of advanced pedagogy. Tertiary's paradigmatic blindness to Shakespeare's philosophy means only a completely new level of education will suffice.

Interested institutions can subscribe to a course of instruction for selected professors and others to begin the process of transitioning from the postmodern malaise into a globally relevant and encompassing natural human practice.

www.ingramcontent.com/pod-product-compliance
Lightning Source LLC
Chambersburg PA
CBHW071402290426
44108CB00014B/1656